Vatican Scandals
and
it's Myths

WARNING
Afraid Of The Truth?
- Then Do Not Read This Book

Printed and bound by
Carraig Print inc. Litho Press
Carrigtwohill, Co. Cork, Ireland.
Tel: 021 4631401

PRINt
IRISH
CLÓBHUAILE
IN ÉIRINN

A catalogue record of this book is available from
the British Library.
ISBN No.: 978-0-9557473-0-4

DEDICATION

This book is dedicated to all people
who search for the truth.
It's dedicated to all those who fight social injustices
for the old, the poor, and the sick,
and for all people in need.
It's dedicated to the brave few who are willing
to live fearlessly to face life head on,
with courage and grit.

Author

John O'Brien received his secondary education at the C.B.S. For the past 20 years he has done a comprehensive study of both the Old and the New Testament. He has developed a profound interest in the only source of truth on God and of his Son Jesus which is the bible. He has studied Countless Biblical aids from all Christian Churches over the same period including hand books, Bible Dictionaries and much more. He has also done a major study on the history of the Popes.

John is an avid reader of all history books. Letters of his on religious issues have been printed by such papers to name just a few, as the Sunday World and the Daily Mail. His book aims to describe the key features of the Christian faith, as outlined in Holy Scripture, and asking questions where necessary.

"According to Pauls custom He went inside to them, And .... He reasoned with them from the scriptures,

Explaining and providing by references that it was necessary for the Christ to suffer and to rise from the dead."

Acts 17: 2, 3

The effect of not believing in God is to believe in anything.

Gilbert K. Chesterton (1874 - 1936)

PREFACE

This book is my effort to share spiritual truth. After many years of diligent study and consulting numerous handbooks, I have found my answers in the teachings of Jesus. I have tried to describe these truths in the language and thought forms understandable to present day people.

Some Christians (what ever their denomination) do not want to discern the truth from the untruth of the Church they serve. It's their choice and perfectly fine by me - as I'm certainly not an evangelist. I am simply a reader of many books - the Bible just being one of them, though the most important.

I set out many years ago to try and find out did I get on this planet through evolution or through a creator. I have after many years of research accepted a creator, if I am wrong it's a one way journey. On death then it will be eternal sleep with all those I've loved.

When I sat down to write this book, I knew that the best work required more ability then I possessed and therefore I needed help that only God could give. This book was written with deep concern for the pain, difficulty and struggle of human existence.

The purpose of this book is a very direct and simple one. It makes no pretence to literary excellence nor does it seek to demonstrate any unusual scholarship on my part. It is written with the sole objective of helping the reader - to be free of false fears and hopes. My aim therefore is to write this book in a logical, simple, and understandable manner.

In mid May 2008 the Vatican astronomer was talking about extraterrestrial life. Joseph Ratzinger through him has endorsed the possibility of other intelligent beings - i.e (extraterrestrial life).

Funnes the Vatican astronomer believes the 'Big Bang' theory was the most "reasonable" explanation for the creation of the universe. This of course would also have to be endorsed by Joseph Ratzinger (Pope Benedict XVI).
Joseph Ratzinger said in 2008 "There are so many

scientific proofs in favour of Evolution which appears to be a reality we can see and which enriches our knowledge of life". The Catholic Church has a long tradition of ecclesiastics who have rejected a literal reading of the bible. Two early church fathers Origen and Augustine were two such ones. Pope John Paul II and Pius XII also spoke up for evolution. In 2005 Christoph Schönborn, Archbishop of Vienna said he had no problem with "Theistic Evolution".

Benedict on the 16th September 2008 said "The theory of Evolution was compatible with the Bible". Vatican 'Theologians', scientists and 'philosophers' are to meet in March 2009 to discuss same. The Vatican as one can see accepts 'Theistic' Evolution*. It's a stand that sees no reason why God could not have used Evolution to create the human species. Richard Dawkins in his book **The God Delusion** said "we on the science side must not be too dogmatically confident".

When I did my psychology course in 1993, I had many questions to ask my tutor on the evolutionary theory. He, a professional psychologist, wrote on one of my exam papers the following; "I have to say the Evolutionary Theory is now regarded as scientific orthodoxy". ALthough he did go on to say "some extravagant claims on it are unwarranted".

Did the world arrive through Evolution? Did humans arrive through Evolution? Many will ask but where did God come from? If through Evolution we arrived, I can ask where did matter come from? If by Evolution when, where, why, and how did life come from dead matter? In his book the **God Delusion**, **Richard Dawkins** says "But the spontaneous arising by chance of the first hereditary molecule strikes many as improbable... maybe it's very, very improbable".

The question of who made God can be answered by simply looking at space and asking "Does space have an end?" Obviously it doesn't. If there is a brick wall with "The End" written on it, the question arises, what is behind the brick wall? Strain the mind though it may we have to believe (have faith) that space has no beginning and no end. The same applies to God, He has no beginning and no end. He is eternal. We understand the concept of Gods eternal nature the same way we understand the concept of space - having no beginning and no end - by faith.

See pages 15-16, 127-128.

* Scientist theologians faced with strong evidence of genetic linkage between homo sapiens and other primates have generated a theory called Theistic Evolution. It says that the development of the human beings progresses much along the lines described by Natural Science, but at a particular point in the development, God imbues humans with the mark that sets them apart from all other species.

FOREWORD

There is a great lot of information in this little book. If a christian or member of clergy - cardinals, bishops, priests etc., it separates truth from myth for you.

If clergy (Roman clergy in particular) some of your teachings are irreconcilable with what the Bible teaches. You still prefer to preach the absurd and erroneous doctrines and ravings of the middle ages.

The primary aim of this absorbing read is to tell you exactly the truth as contained in sacred scripture. Could there ever be anything more important than obtaining this kind of knowledge? But again it's *repeated*, if afraid of such truth or knowledge, please read this book no further.

This book is therefore not intended to be of course anywhere near a comprehensive cover of scandals within the vatican church. The author gets no joy to write about same, however briefly it may be. However he believes to forget or deny injustices of past history increases greatly the chances of same being repeated in the same magnitude.

For instance to forget about the atomic bombs, the Napalm bombs, the concentration camps, the mass murder of helpless people, social injustices of the old and sick, of children, makes it a certainty all to return. Knowing this, the author feels compelled to draw but briefly from **his vast files on * vatican scandals**.

To all who call themselves Christian, do not feel you have to absorb all this book at once. This book does not try to use big words or clever ways of rephrasing questions, in an effort to convince us that the bible is the only source of truth - this book does not have to do that. It's a very personal book, written by someone who believes in God and in the goodness of the world despite its injustices. Certain passages will leap out at once as the truth for you. Work with these first, if I say anything that you disagree with, just ignore it. You most certainly won't need degrees in 'Theology' to understand it, or a 'Masters Degree in Liturgy'.

Truth is something we can all search for and choose, the same way we choose anger, hate or sadness. Christians you will learn later on have **no other source** of truth for spiritual issues, except the doctrines that rest on the authority of sacred scripture. **If sacred scripture is not true, then we are all on a one way journey - on death no more to come.**

We have what are known as five world religions. Christianity, Islam, Hinduism, Buddhism and Judaism. There is however no universally accepted definition of the term "World Religion". Of the five religions listed Christianity has the largest number of followers, an estimated 2.1 billion, followed by Islam with an estimated 1.3 billion.

What makes up Christianity are all the mainstream churches and numerous churches outside main stream. Protestantism, Roman Catholicism* and Eastern Orthodox churches and all Christian churches outside this group are then called the religion of Christianity. The major groups in Protestantism are Baptists, Methodists, Lutherans, Presbyterians, Episcopalians, Quakers etc. The name Protestant originated with the

Second Diet of Speyer (1529). It simply means to "protest". The word "Catholic" simply means universal (as translated from greek).

It's of no concern to the author as to what Christian church you profess allegiance. I deeply respect the longings and aspirations of persons from all Christian churches. I seek to treat each church fairly without wishing to compare them.

I have picked one Christian church (Vatican) to compare it with what the Bible says in this book. I could equally have picked other Christian churches to compare with scripture also. **Some other Christian churches would have similar teachings if not the same as the Roman Catholic one**. They also like the Roman Christian would have their scandals of course.

The ultimate goal of this book is to compare the teachings of Jesus (Christianity) with some from some Christian churches. Book space has only allowed me to concentrate on one church (Vatican). The author has no desire to judge any church, or to favour one above another. **I simply relate years of meticulous research of the Bible** for you. My findings have been corroborated by the most prominent of handbooks, dictionaries (just a few mentioned in this book) and most importantly by all the Bibles.

People have called themselves Christian for many different reasons. Many who do suffer from spiritual delusions. This has been manifested in how so called 'Christians' from different Christian churches treat each other. They kill each other and use so called 'war' etc as an excuse. They will hate each other for skin colour. For many of them their actions reveal them to be "workers of lawlessness" (Matt 7:21-23). Some who call themselves "Born again" are just like Nicodemus - they do not understand what Jesus meant. They have perverted Christian views of themselves.

Broadly speaking *Christianity which again is an estimated 2.1 billion, of which the author is - is the religion derived from the teachings of Jesus. On this all of us will be judged, if we were true or false.

* Note the author frequently refers to the Roman Catholic Church as the Roman Christian in this book. This is done for obvious reasons.

* Vatican scandals will of course mean by its Popes, or Vatican clergy wherever in the world they reside.

* Christianity is open to all world religions. All humans can search for and find Jesus. Jesus died for all humanity. As long as they accept Him - and put faith in his ransom sacrifice and live by His words, they can be saved. The pathway to true Christianity is open to all.

CONTENTS

INSPIRED BY

Joseph Ratzinger

The inspiration to write this book came from Joseph Ratzinger. This man who was once Known as *"Gods Rottweiller"* became Pope Benedict XVI in 2005. Pope John XXIII updated the Roman Catholic Church. He called the second Vatican Council on 25th July 1959. One of the major changes John XXIII made was concerning the Roman Catholic Mass. He changed it from the Latin to the Vernacular. I was glad the Latin Mass was done away with, because I believed now at last I could find out God's Message to me, in a language I could understand.

I remember as an altar boy having to learn my responses to the priest as he celebrated the Latin mass. I hated Latin yet despite this years later I was to get honours in it during secondary school years. But as already mentioned John XXIII brought the Roman Church into the modern era, by the removal of Latin. John was to remain Pope for less then five years. On his death in 1963 he got expressions of sympathy from Jewish, Muslim and Buddhist leaders, and from all Christians around the world.

In 2007 it emerged that Pope Benedict wanted to bring back the Latin Mass. But then again, Benedict and his ludicrous ideas are nothing new. He in January 2008 got the honour of the first Pope, forced to cancel a trip to an Italian university over what they called his *"Reactionary Views"*. The trip was cancelled for *"security fears"* on account of Benedict's views. One Vatican source said *'the tension was getting too much and there were real security fears'*.

On Sunday 14th January 2008 - Pope Benedict turned his back to the congregation as he celebrated some of his mass. Why did he do this? He did it as he celebrated some of the mass in Latin. One paper described it as *"Re-introducing an old ritual that had not been used in decades"*. The paper also said *"Benedict is slowly re-introducing practices phased out after Vatican II."*

In 2007 the former Vatican theologian Pope Benedict XVI made the following ludicrous announcement that according to him Roman Catholic Christians were the only *'true'*

Christians, with him as their head on earth. Such perverted teachings have been responsible for much blood loss, atrocities and abominations throughout the ages. This was the inspiration to write this book. It was only then I began the arduous task of writing this book. After much thought and deliberation I decided to immerse myself writing about the most important book of all, and the truth it contained. In reality the bible talks of two different classes of Christians, some who are true and some who are false or lukewarm.

Either type of Christian would know themselves, if they were true or false. They would know by their deeds or actions or their thoughts. God through John on the Island of Patmos said to the Christians in Philadelphia, The following rev. 3:8 *"I know your deeds - look1 I have set before you an opened door, which no one can shut - that you have a little power, and you kept my word and did not prove false to my name"*. So therefore to be a true christian it's essential not to prove false to God. Jesus said: This means everlasting life, their taking in knowledge of you, the only true God, and the one whom you sent forth, Jesus Christ - John 17:3.

Lets next find out how God views such Christians who are false, Rev. 3:15,16 *"I know your deeds, that are neither cold or hot. I wish you were cold or else hot. So because you are lukewarm and neither cold or else hot, I am going to vomit you out of my mouth"*. Every one of course knows what is meant by that.

The Pope on the other hand believes to be a true christian, all that is required is to have him as your head. If that was the case Hitler and many of his government leaders who were baptised Roman Catholics were some of the *'only true'* christians under Pius XII. Many of the most infamous clergy who were criminals of all sorts had the Popes as their head. Did that in turn make them the only *'true'* christians? One can see how the statement of Benedict XVI is so ludicrous.

The word that God spoke about is of course if you profess to be a christian is the only truth. Man made myths and traditions are of course false. At psalm 119;105 it says *"your word is a lamp to my foot, and a light to my roadway - "* it means without God's word we are in darkness. With it our roadway through life is lit up - we are

4

no longer in darkness. Proverbs 13:9 says *"the very light of the righteous will rejoice; but the lamp of the wicked ones - it will be extinguished.* Jesus said at John 18:37 . . . *"For this I have been born, and for this I have come into the world, that I should bear witness to the truth"*

Of course we can turn our backs on the truth, the option is ours. We can turn our backs on the truth and accept in its place fairy tales and myths. We can turn our backs on Gods words and be ashamed of them, because for now accepting fairy tales and myths may make us feel better. We may want to believe something that's not in God's word, the Bible, because maybe it gives us false comfort and hope.

But what does God say through his inspired word will be the result, if we are ashamed or deny His words of truth? Through His Son Jesus he gives you the answer at Luke 9:26 when it says - "If anyone is ashamed of me or my words, the Son of Man will be ashamed of him when he comes in His Glory of the Father and of The Holy Angels".

Jesus went on to say to would be christians also the following at John 8:31,32. *"If you remain in my word, you are really my disciples, and you will know the truth, and the truth will set you free"*. Jesus also promised for anyone who would listen to his voice the following at rev 3:20. *"Look! I am standing at the door and knocking. If anyone hears my voice and opens the door, I will come into his House and take the evening meal with him and he with me"*.

The Word of God to repeat through his son Jesus is the only truth. So where does one get this only truth? Jesus again clearly gives you the answer at John 17:17. There he says to God concerning his disciplines - *"sanctify them by means of the truth; your word is truth"*. So as every Christian should know the Word of God is the only truth as contained in sacred scripture. 2 Timothy 3:16 says *"all scripture is inspired of God"*.

Popes, Cardinals, Bishops, etc., have no further source of truth. The same source of truth is open to all of us anytime we wish - **in 1994 Cardinal Cathal Daly said *"The Great Renewal of the Church through and after the Vatican council was*** *to a rediscovery of the early church and the early church's experience through the scriptures which was the* **SOURCE OF ALL** *the Church's knowledge on God"*. This report appeared in the Irish Examiner on the first of April 1994.

So the Cardinal tells you ever so clearly if you profess to be a Christian what you should already have known. They have no keys to open any vaults for more secret information on God. It's the Bible and no more - it's there for all to read. So as God's word as Jesus tells you is *"truth"* one can safely conclude then if it's in the bible it's true, if not it's false, a *"Godless myth"*, just a man made tradition. On reading this book it's imperative that you remember this.

Despite what you've been told some of you may want to find this book controversial, as it will go against some of the untruths you've been told as a Christian (from whatever church). So to simply confirm what you've been told as I am certain this will be necessary for some of you, consult the Bible as the Bereans did. The Bereans were new to the Word of God just like you may be. So to know if Paul was telling them the truth or not they examined the scriptures daily to confirm if it was in scripture or not. Do not passively allow others to mold your thinking. Check and see if they tell truth or lies.

The truth allows only for things to be one way. For example, either humans have a soul that survives death or not. Either God will bring wickedness to an end or he will not. These and many other beliefs are either right or wrong. There cannot be two sets of truth when one does not agree with the other. One or the other is true, but not both. Sincerely believing some untruth and practicing that belief, will not make it right if it really is wrong.

How should you feel if proof is given that what you believe is wrong? For example say that you were in a car, travelling for the first time to a certain place. You have a road map, but you have not taken time to check it carefully. Someone has told you the road to take. You trust him sincerely believing that the way he has directed you is correct (without looking at your map) but what about if his way is not the right direction - and someone points out the error?

What if the person who shows you the error also shows it to you on your map that you are on the wrong road? Would pride or stubbornness prevent you from admitting that you are on the wrong road? What if someone through your own Bible shows you are wrong - that you are not on the road of truth that leads to freedom, and as you read at the start proving false to the Name of God? Would you then be willing to change from a broad road of destruction? A road of *"Godless Myths"*. A road that God will *"vomit"* you off at the end. A road of false fears, and uncertainties - or will you still stay on that road? Or will you abandon the broad road as your map tells you it's the wrong one and get on the narrow road to life?

But if you do find this book controversial, you will also have in return to find God's Word controversial. If you profess to be Christian you will also have to find the Word's of Jesus who suffered death for you equally as controversial. You will also have to find the fact that you call yourself 'Christian' from whatever Church controversial. In reality you will have to find Christianity controversial. Because at all times this book quotes directly from sacred scripture.

When it comes to God's Word and commands from Jesus it's the Bible that's quoted at all times. If it's in the Bible it's quoted, not in the Bible it's not quoted.

This book hasn't any interest in attacking the honest convictions of sincere persons. And its purpose is certainly not to disparage such persons. Its purpose again is simply to tell facts from the bible relating to spiritual issues. It tells you exactly what early Christians believed, Christians who broke bread with Jesus, walked the dusty roads with Him to spread the word of God. Did they believe in an immortal soul? Did they believe in purgatory? Did they believe like the Roman Christian Church today that there was a need for an act called 'Transubstantiation'? Did they believe at the appointed words of men that ordinary bread and wine could be turned into the actual body and blood of Jesus?

They were to suffer martyrdom for centuries for their beliefs. The persecutions of early christians began under Nero. Great numbers were thrown to wild beasts, burned alive in the amphitheatres. They were crucified; others covered with the skins of wild animals, and thrust into the arena to be torn asunder by savage dogs, lions, etc. The early Christians were hunted like beasts of prey. So why were all such Christians, many who had talked with Jesus, prepared to suffer martyrdom in the most heinous of ways for?

End Or A Future?

Jean Harlow, Natalie Wood, Bob Marley, Karen Carpenter, James Dean, Brian Jones, Elvis Presley, Marilyn Monroe, Judy Garland, etc. What have the few listed names in common? It was of course like countless others they all died young. The young listed died at the height of their careers, they were some of the brightest entertainers. Have you ever wondered what exactly happened to them once they died?

Perhaps you know the empty feeling that comes with loosing a loved one to death. How very sad and helpless you can feel! It's only natural to ask: what happens to a loved one when they die? Are they still alive somewhere? Will the living ever again enjoy the company of those now dead? Have you ever asked what has happened to the young mother or the young father who died leaving a young family? Are they now in a place, very happy, looking down on perhaps the young family they left behind? Have we not been told this many times by clergy etc.? But have you ever asked how could a young mother who has died be happy looking down on her young family, knowing she has left them, and that they must get on in a big bad world without her?

So what exactly happens at death? Perhaps you believe nothing? Or in the case of the young mother complete *'Bliss'* in a much better place? Simply do you believe all the dead young people are not dead but living *'Eternal Life'* as disembodied souls in Heaven? Do you believe you live on in a vague insubstantial something, called a shadowy immortal soul?

If you are an atheist or a materialist you will already have answered there's nothing to come after death. On the other hand nearly all religionists say we survive bodily death - in one form or another - but is that true? But who ever is right or whoever is wrong one thing though is certain we all die. The Poet was also certain of that when he wrote during World War I.

"I have a rendezvous with death
At some disputed barricade,
When spring comes back with rustling shade
And apple-Blossoms fill the air-
I have a rendezvous with death
When spring brings back blue days and fair".

If we believe in a creator most of us will cling on to hope for the future be it true or false. If we believe in Darwins Evolutionary Theory for man's origins then that goes clearly against the Story of Genesis, it makes a complete myth out of the Genesis Story, and if a Myth is made from Genesis then it in return makes a myth out of all the Bible, you will clearly see why later.

Of course Darwin gets most praise for his particular theory, but it had been put forwarded by many men before him - one in particular Jean-Baptiste Lamarck. In 1871 Darwin made his suggestion: Apes and humans were descended from the same ancestor. Darwins theory of natural selection suggests that all animals and plant species can be traced back to a single common ancestor.

Thomas Henry Huxley became Darwins most outspoken champion - he became known as *"Darwin's Bulldog"* Huxley once said to his wife before a public lecture *"by next Friday evening they will all be convinced that they are monkeys"*. When Huxley confronted Bishop Samuel Wilberforce in a debate the Bishop inquired whether his ape ancestor was on his grandfather's or his grandmother's side, Huxley replied *"He would rather have an ape for a grandfather than a pious hypocrite"*.

The Genesis Story says that man was God's supreme creation and that animals were created for him for companionship. Make a farce out of Genesis and then all the Bible follows to its very last page - make a farce out of Genesis and the Atheist is right, there is no God, life happened by accident - on death there's no prospects of life to follow. That's it, just a one way ticket. 1Corinthians 15:22 says *"Just as in Adam all are dying, so also in Christ all will be made alive"*. Can you see then to dismiss Genesis or to accept: *Evolution is incompatible with Christianity? If we doubt that in Adam all are dying,* how can we hope that in Christ all will be made alive?

So either we want to accept that God created man as told through His inspired word or the evolutionary claim that man himself was an animal. God as the Evolutionists claim simply putting it means that an all powerful and all seeing God needed a roundabout way to make man which goes entirely against Sacred Scripture. But due to the limited pages of this book it's not written to debate creation or evolution. It's written for persons who believe in a creator as Genesis points out - it's written to help you find the truth as contained in Holy Scripture. So again why is truth so important? Again Jesus gives the answer at John 8:32 "Then you will know the truth and the truth will set you free". Most persons like the Buddha want to search for truth and the meaning and purpose of life - we agonise over why we have to grow old and die?

I remember many years ago when in secondary school and during my religious studies I agonised over why I had to die one day? Why I had to loose people in death I loved? I never wanted them to die. I myself all those years ago wanted to live for ever. I of course have never lost that desire, I would still love to live for ever on earth with all my loved ones - as would anyone who has a healthy mind and body.

For think: if you had to decide on what day (date) you choose to die? You cannot pick one, can you? Of course you do not want to die, and neither does any other normal person who has a measure of health. Why would you think this is?

Well the answer is obvious God has created us with the desire to live, not the desire to die. The Bible states this as following at Ecclesiastes 3:11 *"He has put Eternity into their minds"* - so all those years ago I could not forgive Adam that one day on account of him just as I was about to get dug in I was going to die.

So about 20 years ago I again wondered about the meaning of life on earth. I looked at a huge star filled sky, I admired a colourful sunset and the beauty of the countryside. I again reasoned there must be some grand purpose to all these things. I found myself asking once again as in those long ago school days, am I to live just a short time, get what I can out of life and then die? I wanted life to be more then a brief cycle of birth, life and death.

I remembered a story I once read about John Wesley who was caught with fellow passengers during a storm in mid-atlantic. John Wesley was terrified of the storm and afraid to die. John Wesley realised he was afraid of death because he did not know God. So I like John Wesley did not know God's true plan for me. It was from my darkness I slowly studied the bible again with the aid of many biblical aids to support what I had read. It was out of this darkness from not knowing the truth and being like John Wesley I found the truth, and glad to say as Jesus has said it has *"Set Me Free"*.

I would sincerely hope that you too if you are in darkness that you too on reading this book but most importantly of all on reading your Bible will discover the truth and that you too will be set free from false fears. That's the reason this book contains extensive references to the Bible. I believe for man to be trapped by myths is like a man mired in quicksand. He is not likely to free himself from it alone unless he gets help.

We don't want to be like the rich man in the Bible who did not know God. The rich man said to himself *"Soul"* (please note the word *"soul"* for later). *"You have many good things laid up for many years; take your ease, eat drink and enjoy yourself"*. But on that very night this man died. Like a disappearing mist the rich man would pass away before he could see his dreams fulfiled. Again please note that the Bible has the *"Soul"* here eating and drinking and having a good time on earth - much more of this later.

The Early Christian Church

The first Christian Church was founded by Jesus, it was His Church. The Catholic Encyclopedia 1991 states *"In the New Testament the term Church always refers to a group of people"*. Any group of Christians, meeting together regularly, whether in a home, a school hall or in open air is called a Church. The first Church of **true Christianity** established itself at pentecost A.D 30. The first Church was of course led by the Apostles, the disciples of Jesus and their immediate followers.

This apostolic era was noted for its extraordinary missionary expansion of the church by all its apostles. The first Christian Church was in Jerusalem. The first Christians devoted themselves to the apostles teaching in Jerusalem, *"And also to the breaking of bread and the prayers"* Acts 2:42.

From Jerusalem the Church spread outwards. By the close of the century, it was strong in Asia, Macedonia, Greece and Rome. The expansion was largely due to the efforts of Paul, the first Christian missionary. By the end of the 2nd century the Church had spread to the Mediterranean area and France. However success also led to quarrels and disputes which divided and weakened the Church. The Bread issue as in the Last Supper was just a simple meal for Christians. You are told that very clearly at Acts 2:46 when it says - *"Every Day they Continued to meet together in the Temple Courts. They broke bread in their homes and ate together with glad and sincere hearts"*.

We always break bread as Jesus did with his Apostles with our family and friends when we come together for meals. The Apostles moved all over with the christian message - they could move freely around Rome as well for some years due to the "Pax Romana" (latin for Roman peace). It was a period of approximately 200 years, which began with the reign of Augustus Caesar.

Some early christians who were not as yet "true" followers considered themselves not a new religion but rather a Renewal Movement within Judaism. The result was that they still worshiped in the Temple, and continued to observe Jewish Laws. The Bible tells you *"The Disciples were called Christians First at Antioch"* Acts 11:26. True christians of course had no temples, they built no altars, used no crucifixes, only worshiped God as they were told by Jesus. But Paul then as he warned knew that it would change. He warned at Acts 20:29, 30, *"I know that after my departure fierce wolves will come in among you not sparing the flock; and from among your own selves will arise men speaking perverse things"*. The First letter of John Chapter 2:18, 19, 22 also told of Apostasy. A major impact on Apostasy occurred with the early christians when Constantine entered the picture. This led to the start of State Religion disguised as 'Christianity'.

This led to the growth of the so called Holy Roman Empire, and in return developed the power of Christendom's chief religious leaders, the Pope of Rome and the Patriarch of Constantinople, and in return a struggle for supremacy. They both excommunicated each other in 1054, thus the Eastern Orthodox and Roman Christian Church were born. This break was known as 'The East-West Schism'.

THE VATICAN

In the heart of the Roman faith can be found the Vatican, it's the palatial home of the Pope. Popes were firmly established in the imperial city by the sixth century. The Bishop of Rome was declared to be head over his Church. The Vatican is the smallest independent state in the world. It's the governmental centre of the largest Christian Church on earth. The Vatican city covers 108.7 acres (44 hectacres). Vatican city lies entirely within the city of Rome. High stone walls surround most of the city.

It has its' own currency, its' own bankers either dead or alive! The Milan banker Roberto Calvi, took over the role of 'God's Banker' once. Calvi was to become one of the dead bankers - before his time! Around this time Pope John Paul II said he wanted to make the Vaticans financial affairs "clear and in the light of the sun".

Museums and picture galleries abound in the Vatican. It has sculpture galleries, libraries, collections of objects found in ancient ruins, priceless art galleries etc. The Vatican palace is a group of connected buildings with well over

1,000 rooms. It has grand staircases and salons, it has beautiful gardens and private apartments of the Pope. In truth the Vatican has amassed huge wealth. Of course other Christian Churches would also have amassed great wealth. Their heads also live in the same luxury as the Pope.

The Vatican itself employs about 1,300 people, mostly lay people, recruited in Italy. The Vatican city does not have an army capable of fighting a war. But it does have its' own "armed forces". The most famous of these are the Swiss Guards. Swiss guards and German soldiers paraded in front of each other at either side of the white line drawn in front of the Vatican during World War II. The German soldiers could not cross over it.

The Church of Peter, this vast edifice was begun by Pope Julius II in 1506. It took 176 years to finish. Everything connected with Peter was done on a vast scale. It was from the construction of this massive cathedral that the Church began to make merchandise of the Grace of God. The Pope never told the People as Ephesians 2:8 says *"By this undeserved kindness, indeed, you have been saved through faith, and this not owing to you, it is God's gift"* and also at 2 Corinthians 12:9 scripture says *"My undeserved kindness is sufficient for you"*.

But Julius and Popes to follow never told the people that so in order to raise funds for this vast church the sale of indulgences entered the picture. The people were told as soon as the money hit the bottom of the money chest, then the 'soul' who it was paid on behalf would escape from purgatory. Luther was greatly angered by this *"Myth"*. This was one of the causes of the Protestant Reformation. Luther had known from his Bible that the sale of indulgences, was not biblical it was an effort to extort money by playing upon the minds of the superstitious people.

The people were taught not only too look to the Pope as their Mediator, but to trust in acts of their own to atone for sin, long pilgrimages, acts of penances, the worship of relics, the payment of large sums of money to the Church and many similar acts were looked for by the Pope to cover the sins of the people. Had the people possessed the Bible they would not have been so easily deceived. They would have known their sins were covered by Jesus once and for all time for them by His Death on the Cross.

But for hundreds of years the circulation of the Bible was prohibited. People were forbidden to read it or to have it in their homes. To increase the power and wealth of the Pope the bible at all costs had to be withheld from the people. It was all as one can see now for very obvious reasons. Anyone who exposed the unscriptural practices of the Popes, might have indeed met a very fiery end. Thousands of so called Heretics were tortured to death or burned at the stake.

In 1993 an article appeared on a daily paper that said the Vatican Bank called IOR had 2 branches and 3 cash dispensers and that it managed billions belonging to individual clerics and religious bodies, and that was excluding its own vast wealth. That same year in 1993 writing for the Winter issue of studies Gerry Hanlon SJ Dean of Theology at Miltown Institute wrote "The Roman Catholic church has massive resources in property, land and institutions". He also stated "The Church fails to incorporate within its own life the message it preaches." Ireland's homeless champion priest Peter McVerry, spoke of the

Vatican's wealth in December 2007. In the *'Would You Believe?'* documentary, he hit out at his own church for its huge trappings of wealth.

He said "they build big palaces for their bishops and enjoy the status and the wealth like the politicians. This is an enormous distortion of the message of Jesus". McVerry went on to say wryly *"Jesus would turn in his grave if he had not already risen".*

One might be justified in asking any need for the Vatican to beg for money then? The answer is of course yes! The following is one such example. In 1994 the following letter appeared in a Co. Waterford Paper.

It was from Bishop William Lee to His people and some of its contents were as follows *"money from the people for the upkeep of the Holy See".* The Bishop of Waterford and Lismore asked for the people to *"be generous".* He also said *"The demands of the Holy Father are increasing so much that each year the Holy See shows a deficit".* He concluded his letter by saying *"The Holy Father needs our generosity".* William pretended not to know the wealth of his superior.

The first Christians were not asked to pay the "*Tithes*". They were exempt from the Laws of Judaism, they were no longer commanded for instance to keep the Sabbath Day Holy, Jesus by his sacrifice had done away with the Old Commandments. The Christians were discharged from the old system of law. Galatians 4:8-11. Colossians 2:16,17. Romans 14:5. Christians instead have the laws of the "*New Covenant*" to live by. The first christians then were only encouraged to support their elders who travelled from place to place to preach the Gospel.

How The Vatican Became A State?

The Vatican had contact with fascist dictators well before and during World War II. Fascism was the form of Government in Italy from 1922 to 1943 under the leadership of Benito Mussolini. Fascist states were ruled by a dictator with great restrictions upon the freedom of individuals. Such states had extreme Nationalism and Militarism. All opposition to the Fascist governments was rigorously suppressed.

Benito Mussolini was born in 1883. he got involved in Politics from an early age and was often arrested for his activities. He began to believe that the only way to change society was through the use of violence. His fascists attacked Trade Unionists, broke up strikes etc. By 1926 IL Duce (the leader) had become a dictator. His great friend in Germany was of course Hitler. The Duce and Hitler regularly exchanged letters and visits. Hitler had come to Italy to meet Mussolini in 1938.

Three years after Mussolini became a dictator, the Vatican in return by him became a State. In 1870 various states making up Italy were unified

- the Papal states that were the churches preserve since the days of Charlemagne were also incorporated. This led to a conflict between the Vatican and Italy But in 1929 the Pope and the Fascist Dictator signed what was called the Lateran Treaty. The Pope from Mussolini got his own State - The Vatican City. The Vatican also for having some of its land confiscated in 1870, got a vast amount of money as compensation.

Is The Pope Infallible?

Do you believe that the Pope is infallible? If you do in what respects is he unable to err? And what significance does this have for the Roman Christian church? Above all is this teaching based on the Holy Scriptures? Joseph Ratzinger once admitted that the matter had given rise to a *"Complicated Controversy"*. *"Infallibility"* means, then, that the Pope, even though he makes mistakes like all other humans does not err when defining matters of faith and morals Ex Cathedra, (acting in the office of shepherd of the Roman Catholic Church). **Author Stewart Lamont** in his book *Church and State* said the following; "The Pope is believed by Millions of Christians to be infallible in matters of dogma, but has shown that in temporal matters all too fallible.

The Infallibility Doctrine came about in 1870. Cardinal Manning of Westminister with more of the Roman Curia gave their support to it. They decided to bring forward some dogma on infallibility for Pius. During the first Vatican Council of 1870 historical records show some very heated arguments took place between bishops and cardinals like Manning and Paul

Cullen to get this Dogma passed. It was reported some Bishops who were against the Dogma, were silenced by the Howls of the Bishops who favoured it.

Paul Cullen was the first Irish Cardinal. He was born in Co. Kildare. In 1832 he was made rector of the Irish College in Rome. At the first Vatican Council he was responsible for composing the final definition of papal infallibility.

Pius himself wanted it at all costs - if the Council majority were against it, he was prepared to dismiss them and make the "definition" by himself. Historical records reported the Papal Nuncio (Ambassadors) intimidated the Bishops into a majority to accept this Dogma for Pius. But it's true to say the controversies over this Dogma were there for many years following the First Vatican Council.

The Vatican theologians with the Pope come up with the ideas the Pope might want to put forward. If the Pope doesn't like the proposals then they don't get beyond the Vatican walls. Infallibility cannot be bestowed on any human, it is predictable to God alone. Joseph Ratzinger in his role as a Cardinal was responsible for keeping an eye on the theologians for John Paul II. If the theologians spoke out of hand they were summoned before Ratzinger's Congregation to explain their views and to conform to the Pope's beliefs or else.

Hans Kung was one such victim of Joseph. Also a Leonard Buff got his ears clipped and was silenced for his views and forced to resign the priesthood. A bishop in France was also removed from Office. The Pope believes he can modify Divine Law, since his power as he sees it is not from man, but of God.

COURAGE

My attention was drawn to the word courage during my secondary school years with my study of the Shakespearean play Macbeth. Macbeth at the start of this play was called *"Brave Macbeth"*. But later Lady Macbeth had to tell her husband to "screw your courage to the sticking place, and we'll not fail. Milton says of courage its "never to submit or yield". Lord George Goschen (1831 - 1907) once wrote *"I have the courage of my opinions"*. Confucius the great Chinese philosopher and teacher of ethics once wrote "to see that is right and not to do it is want of courage".

To be denounced for cowardice is truly terrible. The Vatican was once denounced for its' "irresponsibility and cowardice". Sadly the word courage is not in everyone's vocabulary. Is your life limited by fear? Facing fear builds confidence and emotional strength, and in return courage. This courage will allow you to make a difference in the world. I took the advice of confucius and wrote a book. I saw what was "right" and did it.

How does the World Book Dictionary define courage? It defines it as following *"as moral strength that makes a person face any danger, trouble or pain steadily and without showing fear"*. Such courage has been written about in fact and fiction stories.

Author Stephen Crane wrote his great classic *"The Red Badge of Courage"*. It's all about Henry Fleming and how his courage left him during a battle of the American Civil War. But Henry was not to remain a coward, he finally proved himself in a later battle a man. He had met death face to face and had found out after all it was nothing but death. No longer was he afraid of death. His head at last high, he was able to wear his red badge of courage with great pride.

The victoria cross and other such medals have been won for battlefield courage but away from the battlefield courage is manifested in many other ways. Elsie Kuhn Leitz was a beacon of courage in the darkness of World War II. The daughter of a famous industrialist, she risked everything to save the lives of those persecuted by the Nazi regime. You have of course both moral and physical courage. For instance it takes courage to speak out. It takes courage to meet with triumph and disaster, and treat both of them the same. It takes courage to hear the truth one has spoken twisted around, and to accept same. It takes courage to watch the things you gave your life to, broken, and then to build them up again.

Courage as stated already is needed to speak out. Bishop Sean Brady in 1995 said *"it's never popular to speak out and sometimes the speaker is not popular either, but he has to tell the message he cannot water it down"*.

It takes courage to express ones convictions. But courage is essential for living, without it we only remain a shadow of our true selves. To be remembered for ones courage is the ultimate in satisfaction. Many the world over are remembered for their courage. Would it not be wonderful to remembered for your courage? Would it not be great to be remembered "as the bravest of the brave?" This was how Napoleon described his Field Marshal Ney.

Ney led the Imperial Guard at Waterloo. The Imperial Guard itself, with Ney at its' head, rolled up the hill time and time again to attack the English squares. Ney, beside himself with rage, a broken sword in his hand, urged the Guard forward. But for this act of courage it was to be too late. After the Battle of Waterloo when Ney was sentenced to death he replied - *"Don't you know sir, that a soldier does not fear death?"* So to show courage in whatever way in ones life is truly commendable. Do you want to be remembered for your *"irresponsibility and cowardice"* as the Vatican was referred to, or for your courage?

Anti-Semitic Scandal

Unfortunately the Vatican has indeed been anti-semitic through the years. This in return has been responsible for much Jewish persecution and bloodshed over the centuries. It's well believed the Vatican in modern times during World War II approved Anti-Semitic measures approved by the French Vichy Government. It was only in 1965 that the Vatican abandoned the teaching of the Jews collective guilt for Christ's Crucifixion. It was only in 1994 that John Paul II and Israel formally established full diplomatic relations.

It was a case of peace calling Christian and Jew home. It was clear that the Vatican should have taken such steps, many years before, as when Yasser Arafat was threatening to drive the Jews into the sea, the hand of friendship from the Vatican was not there. The main reason was that the Vatican always had a problem with Israel, as it always had a problem with Jews!

Passive Resistance and Heroism

The author wishes to state the words passive resistance do not apply to Vatican clergy in general during World War II. Because later as we acknowledge the passive Resistance by Pius XII to Hitler, it must also be acknowledged that during World War II a number of priests were murdered in concentration camps. Many Polish Clergy were murdered after the German Polish War of 1939. Moksymilian Kolbe a Catholic priest from Warsaw gave his life to save a fellow inmate at Auschwitz. However a magazine (Kolbe) published before his arrest had carried anti-semitic material. A Roman Catholic Dean in Berlin protested from the pulpit against the persecution of the Jews, he died on his way to a Concentration Camp.

Only one Catholic Bishop however was expelled by organised, Nazi mobs. The German Theologian Dietrich Bonhoffer put up strong opposition to nazism. His faith and heroism even more then his ideas, made Bonhoffer one of the most influential Christian Philosophers born since 1900. People with little interest in religious matters read and discussed his works. Bonhoffer had fled to America in 1939 to avoid serving in the Nazi Army, but he returned one month later because as a Christian he wanted to take a strong stand against Hitler.

In 1943 he joined a plot to kill Hitler, but was arrested he was held in prison for 2 years, then hanged. He wrote letters and diaries in prison that were published in 1951 in the book *Prisoner for God*. In his book he declared that *"churches were no longer vital to man because they had not condemned Nazism"*. Further proof if it was needed about the passive Resistance of Pope Pius XII against Hitler.

But I would much prefer to be like Bonhoffer to be remembered for my courage then as Pius XII. Bonhoffer like the greatest man who ever lived had paid the ultimate sacrifice of laying down his life for another. At John 15:13 Jesus said of anyone doing such an act the following - *"No one has love greater than this, that a man should surrender his life in behalf of his friends"*.

The following gives an example of what might have been if Pius spoke up. When Hitler sanctioned a programme for euthanasia, a

Catholic Bishop and a Protestant Pastor were able to persuade Hitler he was unwise and the programme was stopped. This only highlights the fact that if only the Pope spoke up what suffering might have been saved. Sadly the Church in Germany through the leadership of Pius also remained a focus of only christian philosophy and therefore only a body of passive resistance to the immoralities of the Hitler regime.

In 1940 Einstein who was Jewish and had no great love of the Vatican, praised the church a little as he believed it was going to make a stance against Hitler. But that praise however little, came long before mass murder of the Jews and others was sanctioned by the Third Reich with no Vatican to denounce it. It came long before Jewish people were burned alive in the crematoria. It came long before soap was made from the fats drained from the murdered bodies. Long before fertiliser was made from the bones of the massacred. Would Einstein have given the Vatican the same praise how ever small it was at the End of World War II?

Of course individual priests, nuns and one monsignor saved pilots and some Jews by hiding them in monasteries and the Vatican. The monsignor was Hugh O'Flaherty - known as the scarlet pimpernel. There's a huge difference in letting the few who found their way to the Vatican hide there from the Nazis and in denouncing the Nazi regime that drove them there in the first place.

In 1994 the Vatican was drafting a document that acknowledged the Church's guilt for fostering anti semitism and failing to stop the Holocaust.

Around the same time Chief Rabbi Meir Lau him self a Holocaust Survivor demanded an "Explicit Apology for the shameful attitude of Piux XII at that time".

Also at that time French Bishops apologised for their silence (the Vatican) during the deportation of Jews and also German Bishops blamed their Church (Vatican) that did not do enough to fight Nazism and condemn the Holocaust.

THE "SILENCE" SCANDAL

Pius XII had succeeded Pius XI in 1939. Pius XII had come from an aristocratic background. Cardinal Eugenio Pacelli became Pius XII on the second of March 1939. Pius XII career before coming Pope was almost entirely in the Diplomatic service for Pius XI. In that position he had found himself in Germany as Nuncio.

So it goes without saying that the future Pope Pius XII had plenty of experience in Germany during Hitler's rise to Power. History books show Pacelli being saluted by a German soldier when, as Papal Nuncio (ambassador) to Germany, he leaves the presidential palace in Berlin, 1929. In the mid 1930's Cardinal Pacelli had travelled to America - and had lunched with President Roosevelt. So before the war and becoming Pope he had lots of International experience and contacts.

Piux XI could indeed have no one better to inform him all about what was happening in Germany during the Nazi rise to power, then his Nuncio Paceli, Pius XII to be. As soon as Hitler came to power in 1933 he was asking for a concordat with the Vatican. Pius XII was in office just before World War II broke out, and never spoke out publicly against the atrocities committed by the Nazis in the War.

Again as noted earlier Pius XI had concluded a concordat with Hitler in 1933 and simply putting it from that time onwards the Vatican became the handmaiden of the Nazi Government. Then as explained Piux XII failed to speak out against the horrors committed by the Nazis in their death camps. The New York Times (first edition, 1941) reported German Catholic Bishops in 1941 at Fulda asking for "War Prayers" for Germany's victory.

The clampdown on Jews by Hitler began almost as soon as the first shots of World War II were fired, so really the Pope had years of notice. Many acts of thuggery were carried out well before the first shots were fired, by Nazi bully-boys in acts of their perceived revenge and in a sadistic manner and once the camps began to be used for human extermination there was no stopping. Concentration camps were nothing new in the thirties, but in early years were not used for mass extermination, people mostly found themselves in there for their beliefs.

But then Hitler a baptised Roman Catholic decided a systematical extermination of Europe's Jews and others would be necessary. Children were almost always gassed first as they were of little use to the Reich. Their mothers then were almost certain to follow. In long wooden huts they were forced to strip, their heads shaved and then marched into giant shower rooms. But instead of water, these humiliated, boney figures were gassed to death.

The Vatican could not deny of course knowing about this human extermination. A little girl who hid away in a warehouse in Amsterdam in 1942 knew about it. Her name was Anne Frank. In her diary she told what the "cruellest of monsters" were doing to the Jewish people and others. Very few escaped from the horrors of Auchwitz. One such man was Rudolf Vrba. The Vatican through him was informed of the extermination of Jews there.

In Italy from May 1942 Jews were obliged to engage in forced and public work. In Rome they laboured under the 'very windows' of the Vatican on the Tiber embankment.

Rudolf Höss said that at Treblinka the victims always knew they were going into the hut to get killed, but he boasted that at Auschwitz they tried to fool the victims until the end. The gas chambers at Auschwitz regularly slaughtered between 6,000 and 12,000 a day. Höss noted that *"the foul and nauseating stench from burning bodies permeated the entire area"*. When allied soldiers liberated Buchenwald they discovered emaciated corpses piled up having been murdered. Reports of the day said liberating soldiers "were sickened" at the sight and when funeral processions for victims of the Nazis at Auschwitz were held in January 1945 they stretched as far as the eye could see.

The author doesn't wish to get into specific horrors committed at the camps, but it's true to say with such persons as Dr. Josef Mengele present they were barbaric and sadistic and evil beyond words. You have already read a Catholic Bishop was able to stop an euthanasia plan, it just boggles the mind as to what the Pope could have spoken up against and stopped.

In 2000 John Paul II asked for *"Forgiveness"* for the wrongs of the Roman Church inflicted on Jews and minorities. On May 28th 2006 Pope Benedict XVI visited Auschwitz, there he asked "Why Lord did you remain silent?" He also asked *"How many questions arise in this place?"* So in reality even *"God's Rottweiller"* was turning on God, by trying to state it was "Gods Silence" and not Pius XII silence who had allowed the barbaric mans inhumanity to man go without denouncing. There of course was no mention of the Vatican's anti semitism policy over the years, which had opened the gate to the huge persecution of Jews. This moved John Paul to ask for forgiveness, as already mentioned, in 2000.

In 1995 people had celebrated the 50th anniversary of the liberation of the concentration camps. As they quietly walked through the desolate grounds they struggled to fathom the enormity of the crime. Some 1,500,000 people had been killed in this camp at Auschwitz where they stood. People had haunting questions that echoed in the cold ovens. The empty barracks with the undisturbed mountain of plundered shoes off murdered people. I also tried to understand the enormity of the crime on my visit to Mauthausen (Austria) in 2006. The Mauthausen Concentration Camp was set up at the quarry site. I walked the "death staircase". Many fell from this staircase (to their deaths). When I entered the Mauthausen museum - I was afterwards haunted by questions and by the photos I had seen. Again Hitler was a baptised Roman Catholic as were many of his government - how could the Vatican have remained silent?

History books show photos of Cardinal Gasparri and Mussolini sitting side by side to mark the signing of the Lateran Pact in 1929. The result was the man that followed Pius XI was prepared to do very little to offend Hitler and the Fascist dictators of the day including Mussolini and the Croatian leader Ante Pavelich. Catholic Croatia was a fascist puppet state. Pavelich was leader of Croatian Catholics who were in an organisation called the Ustashe. Pius XII twice admitted Ante Pavelich into the Vatican when Pavelich was in Rome.

When Pius admitted Pavelich to the Vatican, he already knew of the Ustashe Regimes Massacre of Jews, Gypsies and Orthodox Serbs.

The Ustashe had sided with Hitler, they had massacred 60,000 Jews, 26,000 Gypsies and 750,000 Orthodox Serbs. Pavelich was a fanatical hater of Serbs and at that time was in political exile in Italy, where from he led the Ustashe in their brutal campaign. *"A good Ustashi"* he told his men *"Is he who can use his knife to cut a child from the womb of its mother"* the Ustashe chopped of victims noses, ears, breasts, limbs and of course heads. They poured salt into their wounds, gouged out eyes and buried or burned people alive.

..

GENOCIDE BY CLERGY SCANDAL

The word Genocide was coined in 1944. It is a combination of a greek word meaning ("race", "group" or "tribe") and a latin word cide (meaning "killing"). In 1948 The United Nations defined just what was meant by the word Genocide. It was defined as acts committed with intent to destroy, in whole or in part, a national, ethnic, racial, or religious group. (In times of war or peace).

Genocide by clergy will mean by Vatican priests in this chapter. It will mean priests either dead or alive who participated in acts of genocide. All such priests were ordained by the rites of the Vatican. Such priests could only exercise their ministry only in dependence on their Bishop and in Communion with him. They all made a promise of obedience to their Bishop on ordination - and in return got a kiss of peace from him. The Vatican would then want you to believe no matter what such priests did (in this case genocide) they still remained or remain 'Priests'. They want you to believe the character imprinted by ordination is forever, and that their priests (no matter what they do) are marked permanently by it.

During World War II in the Balkans a Roman Catholic priest led Croat Fascists in an Act of Genocide. The priest was from Petricevac. He led Croat Fascists armed with hatchets and knives to a village where they butchered 2,300 serbs, including 500 women and children. Pavelich the visitor to the Vatican as you have read about in the previous chapter did the same, through the Ustashe. It helps us to understand why John Paul II in 2003 had to beg forgiveness for the Vaticans role in the Bosnia bloodshed.

In 2007 a Vatican priest was sentenced to life in prison for his part in Argentina's *"Dirty War"*. He participated in homicides, torture, and kidnappings. All this happened during the years of violence that gripped the country under a brutal dictatorship from 1976-83. The priest by the name of Von Wernich had conspired with police to get information from prisoners while pretending to give them 'spiritual advice'.

In 1994 a Roman Catholic priest participated in genocide in Rwanda. The Vatican priest was named Athanase Seromba. He was found guilty of horrible acts, and sentenced by the courts. A national paper of the day reported that dozens of Roman priests and nuns may have participated in this Rwandian Genocide. Later a Roman Catholic nun was jailed for 30 years for aiding mass murder there. She had helped militias kill hundreds of people who had been hiding in a Rwandian hospital. The hospital ran red with the blood of the butchered. It was to be many years later that John Paul II only broke his silence and referred to this genocide as *"faults"* of his clergy.

Pius XII you've learned was one who failed to break the sound of silence during World War II. Rudolf Höss commandant at Auschwitz was born into a strict Catholic family. Pius was then as he believed the spiritual 'Head' of the Höss family. When various academics were incarcerated at Auschwitz - "representatives" of Pius voiced objections - Höss acted on this, some were released. History books do not record the "representatives" voicing objections to Höss about Jews and others.

Pius XII spoke from the balcony of the Vatican Palace (at end of war), rejoicing that "thanks to the

goodwill of both sides, Rome (Vatican) has been saved from the horrors of war". Of course horrors had been committed in Rome (one such horror was the Adreatine Massacre) but the Pope closed his eyes to it and similar acts. Why didn't Pius stand on the same balcony during the war to denounce Höss and many like him for cruel sadistic murder?

Author Howard J. Langer who has carried out extensive research into World War II wrote "The genocide of the Jews was carried out with remarkable ease. It was accepted by world leaders who chose to look away; Pius XII was one of them. The pontiff had enormous influence which he chose not to use". The above was included in Howard's book called **The World War II 100**.

In his book **The Holocaust** (1981) Seymour Rossel said "Above all the Jews hoped that the Pope, the most prominent Christian leader, would publicly declare his support for the Jews (and others) and condemn the Nazi killing programme. This the Pope was never willing to do".

HOLOCAUST DENIAL SCANDAL

A Vatican clergyman in 2009 denied the holocaust. He said "There was not one Jew killed by the Nazi gas chambers during World War II." He said it was all "Lies, lies, lies". He said only 300,000 died in the camps. Bishop Richard Williamson was the man who shared this repugnant view with the world. It's important to add the Vatican Bishop is not alone in denying the Holocaust. This extremist view is punishable by imprisonment in Austria and in Germany.

Holocaust when translated from the Latin Holocaustum, means complete destruction by fire, especially of animals and humans. Romanies and Jehovah witnesses and others were also murdered in the camps of course. Rudolf Höss had a great fondness for the witnesses - he in his book described them as "wonderful beings". Himmler was also fascinated by their faith.

As Christians they had refused to kill people (by enlisting in the German army) - for their Christian stance they were incarcerated in the camps. For this they were to die as early

Christians. Laurence Rees in his book ***Auschwitz*** said "The Jehovah Witnesses were the only category of prisoner in the camps who simply had to sign a declaration form to save their lives - the majority did not".

Bishop Williamson in question here had been excommunicated by the Vatican in 1988. When John Paul II excommunicated Richard Williamson, it was not for his repugnant views of the holocaust - but because he was a member of a breakaway group, the society of Pius X.

However todays Pope (2009) the German born Joseph Ratzinger has cancelled Richard's excommunication - as part of his 'duty' to bring all back to the Vatican church. The clergyman that denied the holocaust has been described by a colleague as "intellectually arrogant". A colleague also said Richard Williamson is "obviously a very angry man".

Abuse By Clergy

The author refused to write about clergy put on trial for abuse or alleged abuse (from past or present times from his files). He also refused to name the Cardinals and Bishops in this book who were caught red handed as they covered for themselves and other clergy. This was done on Christian principles. 1 Kings Chapter 8, verse 46 (1 Kings 8:46) says "**For there is no one that does not sin**". Romans 5:12 says "Death come to all, because all sinned" (it was for this reason Jesus died for us all). So God's inspired words (sometimes from Jesus' own mouth) tells us clearly we are all "sinners" in one way or another. Deny this we deny what Jesus spoke and in return God.

All of us "sinners" *once* we repent and have faith in the ransom sacrifice of Jesus are forgiven . Jesus said at Luke 15:7 "I tell you that there will be more joy in heaven over one sinner that repents, then over ninety nine righteous ones who have no need for repentance".

Injustices (abuse) can be directed towards all. It does not mean of a sexual nature in many cases. Dictionaries for instance define slavery as abuse. To use harsh and insulting language towards another is called abuse. Harsh or severe treatment of young or old is called abuse (or social injustices).

Many have been wrongly accused of all types of abuse. Some wrongly accused are sometimes exonerated - sometimes they remain victims of blind justice. Books are full of miscarriages of justice. The most famous army case of miscarriage of justice - would have been the Alfred Dreyfus case. Alfred a Jew was wrongly accused of selling his nations secrets to Germany. The Guilford 4 and the Birmingham 6 are all miscarriages of justice. These are the horrifying crimes committed all in then name of 'justice'.

"Key" To Happiness

Two great American presidents have been mentioned in this book. One of them received the Nobel Peace Prize in 1920, that man's name Woodrow Wilson. Woodrow began his career as a lawyer, but soon turned to teaching. It was not until 1913 he became President of America. On reading the back cover one will notice Woodrow told where the source of true happiness was.

The 16th President of America also knew where the source of true happiness was to be found, you will find out what he said later on in this book.

I studied psychology as noted earlier in 1993. It was my relentless search for knowledge and true happiness. I was doing bible research for a number of years before 1993. It was only as years went by I discovered the Bible was the greatest psychology book ever written. It alone as Woodrow Wilson said - was the key to true happiness.

The Bible points the reader to the finest source of counsel and guidance for all problems. The Bible shows that the inner person is more important than the outward appearance. With true Bible knowledge we find happiness in the face of adversity. It certainly tells us that there is a source beyond human wisdom, that must be looked to for direction and happiness.

The Bible (the inspired words of God) is a best-seller, the most widely circulated book in all history - no other book in history has even come close to the Bible circulation figures. But is the Bible just a book of myths? Did Jesus ever live and die for us? Roman historians mention Jesus, although their references to Him are meagre. Is it possible that these 'eye witnesses' testimonies were false? Early secular historians would have no cause to do that. Tacitus, Pliny the younger, Flavius Josephus all mention Jesus. So even opponents of Christianity never doubted the historicity of Jesus. Richard Dawkins in his book **The God Delusion** (2006) admitted "Jesus probably existed". In 2002, an editorial in the Wall Street Journal stated: "Most" scholars barring the stray atheist have already accepted Jesus of Nazareth as a historical person.

Could 'wise guys' have written all the Bible and the Gospels just to amuse themselves, and con the rest of humanity? To such sceptics historian Will Durant said, "that a few simple men should in one generation have invented so powerful and appealing a personality, so lofty an ethic and so inspiring a vision to human brotherhood, would be a miracle far more incredible than any recorded in the Bible". The Bible runs in harmony throughout.

Apparent discrepancies in the Bible prove that the writers were truly independent witnesses. The Bible is not a book of science, but it is not at variance with any scientific fact. Some of its statements show a knowledge of the world of science which the writer could not have had apart from divine revelation. Archeological evidence has also backed up the evidence of some of those mentioned in the Bible. The Moabite Stone, The Nabonidus Chronicle and much more all confirm the ancient writings.

So persons can safely conclude that Jesus did live, and the Bible is the inspired word of God. To find true happiness we again must live by such words. We must not be like the self 'righteous' pharisees, Jesus despised them for letting on to be so. We have to love not hate. We have to show mercy and forgive. We as "sinners" are not to judge anyone. Jesus at Luke (6:37) said "stop judging and you will by no means be judged". The Bible tells us about all the destructive emotions that can (if unchecked) destroy our happiness, anger, hate, jealousy, unable to forgive and so on. It tells what will give true happiness (and thus we become true Christians (not lukewarm) love, humility, forgiveness and so on.

The Bible tells us where to find help for all problems such as if we are afraid and fearful - at Psalm 56:3,4 it says "when I am afraid I will trust in you. In God whose word I praise, In God I trust; I will not be afraid. What can mortal man do to me? On needing sleep the Bible tells us at Psalm 4:8 I will lie down and sleep in peace, for you alone, O Lord, make me dwell in safety.

If bereaved the Bible tells us to check Psalm 23. If depressed or discouraged it tells us to check Romans 8:28-39. If friends fail it tells us to check Psalm 41 9-11. Lonely, check Psalm 23, troubled, Psalm 107:1-31. For all pains we suffer as humans the Bible (Gods word) has the answers -

from this we get true happiness. Truly the Bible is the greatest psychology book of all time - and as Woodrow Wilson said the "Key" to our happiness.

Do You Call Roman Or Orthodox Priests 'Father'?

For Roman priests this custom had its' origins in Ireland and it was only as Irish people immigrated during the Great Famine years and later that this custom went with them. Then resulting from that, it spread to all English speaking countries. It was helped along by Cardinal Manning you have read about previously in this book when it came to calling the Pope 'infallible'.

The term Father is used in various senses as in head of the household, a founder of class or profession, a founder of a nation. Brazil's dictator Vargas (1883-1954) was for instance known as the *"Father of the Poor"*. Chaucer was known as the Father of English Poetry. Washington as the Father of his country. Christian teachers and writers from the 2nd to 5th centuries, Fathers of their Church. But more importantly God as creator is called *"Father"*. But applying *"Father"* to men as a formalistic or religious title was forbidden by Jesus. So resulting from that it's either right or it's wrong to call men in the spiritual sense Father?

Persons from the Roman Christian Church, and the Russian Orthodox Christian Church call their priests Father. Instead of a Pope or Archbishop as its leaders, the Orthodox Church has patriarchs (Father - Rulers). Orthodox Church means 'right teaching' church. They claim to keep much closer to the teaching of the Apostles then the Roman Christian Church. The Russian Churches contain no statues. Instead they have what's called ikons, painted on wood in beautiful colours.

The teaching of Jesus was; "And do not call anyone on earth father; for you have only one father, and He is in Heaven" Matthew 23:9 . There it is crystal clear for you. Jesus was of course talking about calling some one father in the spiritual sense. The Vatican will say Jesus was only rebuking the pharisees for their pridefulness - but of course that is not true.

On the day in question Jesus was not talking to the pharisees then but was actually talking to his Apostles and the crowds about the pharisees. It was later that day He spoke to the pharisees, which he called *"Hypocrites"*, *"Blind Guides"*, *"Snakes"* etc. Then Jesus asked them how could they escape Gehenna? Of course some bibles use the word Hell here. But from your study on the chapter Hell, you will know of course it's wrong.

Jesus was telling His disciples and the crowd, about how the scribes and pharisees, liked the most prominent places at evening meals etc. They liked to be addressed with titles etc. It was then Jesus told the people listening to Him to make certain they called no one Father in the *"spiritual sense" except God of course. He reminded them all they were all "spiritual brothers"*.

LIMBO

If I told you in the Middle Ages no such place as Limbo existed - would you have believed me do you think? The Pope certainly would not have liked it. The thought that I was doing away with Limbo and it being a nice little money earner for them would have been too much for the Vatican to bear. They would have summoned me before the Inquisition, and then it was recant my views or else! The Vatican could not live with the thought of the impact this truth would have had on its coffers.

Its inconceivable that well into modern days that people still believed limbo existed, as it was a medieval theology. Theologians came up with the myth that it was a place reserved for the dead who deserved neither to see God or eternal punishment. It survived into modern times thanks to the Vatican. The Vatican as usual never did anything to denounce its little money earner. Pope Benedict did say it's no longer there in 2008.

PETER FIRST POPE (PRIMATE BISHOP) ?

The 'Site' of Peters martyrdom has been drawing pilgrims for many years. In his pre-Christmas message of 1950 Pius XII announced that the apostles tomb had been discovered. Ludwig Kaas discovered the 'Bones' of Peter in an excavation that lasted from 1939 - 1949. Later the bones were discovered to be from two men (one young and one much older). Also from a woman, a pig, a chicken and a horse!

The Vatican says a humble fisherman became the first Primate Bishop of Rome. Is there Bible evidence to sustain that Peter was ever in Rome? Peter was a humble man and was not certainly seeking glory. Jesus at Luke 14:11 had told his apostles *"who ever exalts himself will be humbled"*.

So Peter of course did not want any exalted position, and knew instantly what to do when Cornelius who did not know better at that time fell on his knees before Peter when he entered Cornelius home. Peter Instantly lifted up Cornelius telling him - as acts 10:26 tell you - *"Stand up I too am only a man"*.

Peter had obviously listened to Jesus carefully and his words to all the Apostles. Peter the humble fisherman that after the *"Rock"* incident was as yet to deny Jesus three times. Peter who was once a coward, knew who the *"Rock"* was through the *"Father"* (God). He was to make this quite clear when at 1 Peter 2:8, he called Jesus Christ *"Rock"* look up your Bible for that, and while you are at it look and see who Paul called the "Rock". For this you must go to 1 Corinthians 10:4 - there Paul calls Jesus clearly the *"Rock"*, Peter from his own mouth not once in the Bible called himself leader of the apostles.

This is quite obvious at Peter 5:1 when he says "To the elders among you, I appeal as a fellow elder" Peter as one can see was simply a fellow elder. Paul confirmed they were all equal at Galatians 2:9 when he said, *"James, Peter and John those reputed to be pillars"*. Again clear evidence if any more was needed all were equal.

At acts 16:4 it reads *"As they travelled from town to town they delivered the decisions by the Apostles and Elders in Jerusalem."* The only place we know that Peter was for certain was again in Jerusalem and Asia Minor. Can you see what the above means as written by Paul? If Peter was head or the *"Rock"*, who would have made the decisions? Peter of course! But the decisions were made by them all. So we know Peter was in Jerusalem as a *"fellow elder"* for a number of years. Paul visited him there after 3 years, and again from that date 14 years later. It appears Peter was then fairly happy to stay in Jerusalem, until Herod Agrippa executed James. Peter then after his miraculous escape from prison left Jerusalem for *"Another Place"* Acts 12:17.

We know Peter paid little visits to Antioch and Corinth. Peter said himself he was an Apostle to the Churches in Pontus, Galatia and Asia, Cappadocia - but not one mention of Rome. And even if "Babylon" he mentioned was in actual fact Rome, that did not still make him primate Bishop there, no more then it did in Jerusalem. Resulting from one word *"Babylon"* Peter used in his first letter - the Vatican want you to believe it was Rome to try and give some little support to their claim at least.

But again they have not one shred of evidence that Peter ever set foot in Rome. Peter wrote two letters the first was addressed to persons in the

Asia Minor area - it logically follows that the source of the letter *"Babylon"* was the literal place by that name. There's not even a hint of evidence in the Bible to say *"Babylon"* as used by Peter was a cryptic reference to Rome. Both Rome as ancient Babylon were both full of iniquity. In the Bible Rome is referred to in nine verses, not one of them says Peter was there.

As the vicious persecution of Christians by Nero had not as yet begun, even if Peter had been in Rome, there would have been no reason for Peter to veil the identity of Rome by the use of another name. When Paul wrote to the Romans, sending greetings by name to many in Rome, he omitted Peter. Had Peter been a fellow elder there not alone a leading overseer, this from Paul would have been a hugely unlikely omission. Also Peter's name is not included among those sending greetings in Paul's letters written from Rome - Ephesians, Philippians, Colossians, 2Timothy, Philemon and Hebrews.

So what did Peter say at 1 Peter 5:13? He said the following *"she who is at Babylon, who is likewise chosen, sends you greetings; and so does my son Mark"*. What could Peter have meant?

Was *"Babylon"* a cryptic reference for Rome? Was Peter a *"she"*?

Peter was telling fellow Christians, that the Christian Church at Babylon was sending its greetings to them. We may assume if we wish that Peter was himself at Babylon at that time. But as it was the Church that was sending its greetings through Peter, he could equally have been anywhere else in Asia Minor.

The first Christian Church departed from Jerusalem shortly before the Jewish war with Rome 66-70Ad. The first Christian church had started here on the day of Pentecost. The first and most influential of all Christian Churches simply faded from the pages of history. Paul says at Galatians 2:7 that he was entrusted with the task of preaching the Gospel to the Gentiles, just as Peter had been to the Jews, clearly makes Paul and Peter equal doesn't it? And further to that at Galatians 2:11 Paul said *"when Peter came to Antioch, I opposed him to his face"*. Hardly what Paul could have done if Peter was his head, now is it? And why did Paul oppose Peter? Paul gives the answer, it was because *"Peter was clearly in the wrong"*.

And most importantly if Peter was the 'Rock' then of course the dispute that arose between the apostles, as to which one of them was the greatest would not have been necessary. It was obvious that the apostles did not understand Jesus' statement to signify that Peter was their leader (Rock) hence the dispute. Luke 22:24. So most certainly Peter was not the first 'Pope' nor was he known as a *"Primate Bishop"*, all the elders were equal. It was only as times passed that the elders began to call themselves Bishops. From the beginning of the 3rd century Bishops began to function in a more monarchial system, in time the Bishop of Rome claiming to be a successor to Peter was acknowledged, and then afterwards called Pope.

The title 'Pope' is from Greek Papas Meaning Father. By that stage as 2:7 John had warned many deceivers had gone out into the world. Then as Timothy 4:7 mentioned *"Godless Myths"* were getting established. As Romans 1:25 says *"They exchanged the Word of God for a Lie"*. And finally for now on Peter as 1st Pope Paul at 1 Cor 11, 12, 13 says *"My Brothers some from Choloe's household have informed me"* what had Paul been informed? It was as following - Paul said *"One of you say I follow Paul, another I follow Apollos another I follow Peter".*

Now as first century christians if they had one true leader, well obviously they would follow that man. It was a clear opportunity for Paul to say concerning Peter if indeed Peter was their leader. Hold on a moment it's Peter you must follow. But what did Paul say? He simply said *"was Paul crucified for you"?* Clearly he meant Jesus was crucified for them all, Jesus was their head, Jesus was their only leader, he was the founder of their Christian Church and the only leader it would ever need.

The "Rock" Story As It occurred

In the Bible as stated previously in this book all references to the word "Rock" apply to both God and His son Jesus as one might expect. At Psalm 18:2 it says "the Lord is my Rock". As you already know Jesus is called the "Rock" several times. The Rock story came about at Caesarea Philipi. There Jesus asked his disciples "who do people say I am?" His disciples answered some say"John the Baptist, others Elijah", but then Jesus wanted to know who his disciples thought he was? Soon it would be Peters' turn to show faith and speak up for all the Apostles.

Before that let's look at name changing in the Bible. God changed Abraham's wife from Sarai to Sarah. He changed Jacob's name to Israel, after Jacob struggled with the angel. The name Israel means "struggles with God". The Israelites when under Greek or Roman culture, were sometimes given two names, one Hebrew and one Greek or Roman. Paul as a Romas citizen had two names, Saul was his Jewish name.

Jesus nicknamed The Apostle Simon "Cephas" or "Peter". Peter comes from the Greek Pe'tros.

Pe'tros when translated means "a piece of rock, a detached stone or boulder", in contrast to Pe'tra which translates "a mass of rock". Note the huge difference. Barabbas in the Bible when translated means "Son of a Father" Deborah's name in Hebrew meant "Bee". Leah in the Bible translates into "Wild Cow". Caleb in the Bible means "Dog".

Simon was a common name in Bible times. Luke 7:44 speaks of Simon the Pharisee. Acts 8:9 tell of Simon the Sorcerer. Did you know the Apostles had two called Simon? Did you know they had two called Judas and two called James? You had Judas (also called Thaddaeus) also Judas Iscariot. Judas Iscariot was son of Simon Iscariot. One James was called "James the less" to distinguish him from the other. The Apostle Nathanael was also called Bartholomew.

At Caesarea Philipi Jesus was asking all His Apostles who they thought He was - it was not directed to Peter alone. "Simon Son of Jonah", you will learn, answered for them all. It's almost a certainty both Simons were present. It was an ideal time for Jesus to use the nickname Pétros to distinguish both Simons. It's very important to remember after His resurrection Jesus again called Peter, "Simon son of Jonah (John)" no nickname used. Just to note the Apostle Thomas was also called "Didymus".

So as one can see most names translate in something that the person is not literally or expected to be of course! Peter's faith had left him on different occasions. It had left him before and after the "Rock" story at Caesarea Philipi, it had left him during the storm on the sea of Galilee. Jesus said to Peter here "O Man of little faith, why do you doubt? (Matt 14:31) It had left him in the courtyard of the Sanhedrin, when Peter, vigorously denied that he was an apostle of Jesus, while Jesus was being insulted and abused. This was well after the story at Caesarea Philipi. It was only at Pentecost with the descent of The Holy Spirit, that Peter got back his courage.

So when the apostles were asked by Jesus who they thought he was, Peter's faith on this occasion through God allowed him speak up. It was the revelation by the Father in heaven to Peter (as Jesus acknowledged Matthew 16:17) that allowed Peter to know who Jesus really was. This fits in with Matthew 11:27, which says "no man knows the Son, but the Father". The true identity of the Son was hidden, until revealed by God to Peter.

Jesus then said to Peter "Happy (or blessed) you are Simon son of Jonah" for knowing who he was through God. The context of the question at Caesarea Philipi to the disciples was the identification of God's son. At that very moment Jesus was talking to his disciples about God (his Father). The next moment he said "Thou art Peter, and on this rock I will build my Church". The "Rock" of course was God the Father, who Jesus praised the moment before. It was all about God's revelation on that day.

Jesus said to Simon "Thou art Pe'tros, and upon this Pe'tra I will build my Ecclesia (Church). Note it was to be the church of Jesus. Colossians 1:18 says He (Jesus) is the head of the body, the Church. (The Congregation) Now either Jesus is the head of His Church ("My Church") or not. He has told you so of course.

So the head of the Christian Church for all time is Jesus. And it was built on the Pe'tra (translates a mass of rock). Had Jesus been referring to himself objectively or Peter as the

Rock, he would of course said - "upon me" or "upon myself" or as in Peter's case "upon you" or upon thee". If Peter was to be the "Rock", normal form of speech would require Jesus to say of course - Thou art Pe'tros and upon thee I will build my Church.

But what Jesus said at Caesara Philipi, leaves absolutely no possibility of this expression to mean that Christ would build his Church on Peter. Only the most wilfully ignorant or perverted manipulators of the words of Jesus, could twist his speech to imply such a thing. Some of the reigning Popes (as anyone who has studied history will know) practiced vice and all types of sin without restraint. The palaces of some of the Popes were scenes of the vilest debauchery. Just imagine if the Christian Church had been resting on them, and they were its' "rock" or foundation.

Most of the references to "Rock" in the figurative sense in the bible refer to God the Father. But Jesus is also referred to as a rock by Peter at 1 Peter 2 : 8. Also by Paul at 1 Corinthians 10 : 4. Peter of course as one can see called Jesus a "Rock". In other parts of the bible "Rock" symbolises in a general way, a place of safety, protection and refuge.

Again as before Pe'tros in Greek means a piece of rock, but is used as a **proper "name"**. Pe'tra (feminine gender) differs from the Greek Pe'tros (masculine gender) and designates a rock mass ("Rock"). Rock mass refers to God and Jesus at all times in the Bible.

The "Rock" again at Caesarea Philipi was of course God, this "Rock" had just revealed Jesus to Peter and the rest of the disciples in turn. So it was on this "Rock" that Jesus praised on the day and loved that He would build his Church. Jesus said the gates of **Hades (Hell)** which means the grave, would not prevail against it. All this will be explained later. Caesarea Philipi had a sanctuary built to the Pagan God Pan, so it was a good place for Jesus to tell his Apostles, that true Christians would survive paganism and death.

So the Church of Christ was to be built on the "Rock" foundation of the Father. Deuteronomy 32:4 says of God - "The Rock perfect in His activity". 2 Samuel 23:3 says of God "The God of Israel said, To me The **Rock** of Israel spoke". 2

Samuel 22:3 says "My God is my **Rock**" Psalm 62:2 says of God "Indeed He is my **Rock** and my salvation - and most importantly Psalm 18:31 asks, **"Who is a Rock, except our God?"**.

The keys to the kingdom (note *not* keys of Peter) were used by Peter to open up God's Kingdom to different classes of people. Peter used "one key" as it were to open the Kingdom to repentant Jews, another for the uncircumcised gentiles, which the centurian Cornelius was one. Peter also opened to the Samaritans. Paul also used keys as it were - Galatians 2:8 says " For God who was at work in the Ministry of Peter as a Apostle to the Jews, was also at work in my Ministry as an Apostle of Gentiles".

So now you understand what the keys meant, and from your Bible you will note both Peter and Paul in turn opened the Kingdom to the Gentiles with their keys. The bind in heaven and loose on earth etc. was given to all the disciples - it was rules on forgiving ones brother - again all disciples got this Matt. 18:18, and thus it passed to all Christians.

MUST A CHRISTIAN GO TO MASS?

The Catechism of the Roman Christian Church says "On Sundays and other days of obligation the faithful must go to Mass", "those who fail commit a grave sin". So must Christians do this to be saved as it were?

The World Book dictionary defines mass as following as *"the main religious service of worship in the Roman Catholic church"* it defines the Holy Eucharist then as *"a sacrifice"*. But do you need the 'Holy Eucharist' as a sacrifice?

Paul at Hebrews 9:25 tells you with crystal clarity the following. He says, ***"Nor did Jesus enter Heaven to offer himself again and again the way the high priest enters the most Holy Place every year with blood that is not his own"***. God's inspired writer was telling you, Jesus was not to be offered again and again (as in the man made 'Eucharist'). That clearly tells you Jesus suffered in agony for you to his death, to offer the only sacrifice that was ever again needed for you as a Christian. He suffered an excruciating death just for you.

Jesus had done away with the sacrifices of the old priesthood, they were no longer needed. No more sacrifices from old or new were needed. As Paul tells you clearly *"there was no need for Jesus to offer Himself again and again, Jesus entered Heaven **once and for all time**"*. Jesus, paid the ultimate sacrifice by his shed blood.

Paul tells you at Hebrews 9:26, He says,

If Jesus had to offer Himself again and again, then Christ would have had to suffer many times since the creation of the World.

Romans 6:10 says *"Jesus gave Himself as a ransom for all men"*.   That simply means Jesus was crucified for you as the ransom sacrifice for your sins. It was one sacrifice for all time. Hebrews 7:27 says of Jesus;

Unlike the other High Priests, he does not need to offer sacrifices day after day, first for his own sins and then for the sins of the people. He sacrificed for their sins once for all when he sacrificed Himself.

Please remember the words *"once for all"*.

One Sacrifice for sins for all time, none ever again needed. In Old Testament times priests and prophets were mediators for mankind with God. but then in the new Testament the greatest sacrifice of all, achieved Reconciliation between God and Mankind. Jesus through his death had replaced the old mediators. He also had replaced what was called the old covenant of the Old Testament with the New Covenant of the New Testament. Paul said at Hebrews 10:11,

> *Day after Day every priest stands and performs his religious duties; Again and again he offers the same sacrifices, which never take away sin.*

Paul was simply saying any sacrifice like the old priests made was all in vain. No old priesthood was needed, no new priesthood was needed, they could never take away sin, only one priest could do, and thankfully did do that, Jesus. **Hebrews 7:21 tells you *"Jesus is a priest forever"*. You are saved through the everlasting priest Jesus, no other priest can do it. Hebrews 7:25.**

What Is Communion?

The World Book defines communion as following as the "Act of Sharing" also as "The act of Sharing in the Lords Supper, as part of the Church worship; Holy Communion; *Eucharist." A Communion in the Days of Jesus was simply an act of coming together and sharing a meal. It was also known as a "Breaking of Bread". The communion or breaking of bread was done for lots of different occasions in the time of Jesus. It was done for marriages etc.

Most importantly Jesus requested His Apostles to come together in memory of His death and share such a meal in an act of friendship. But hundreds and hundreds of years later from what was just to be a simple commemorative meal for Jesus, was changed for Roman Christians by an act called 'Transubstantiation', more on that later. But firstly back to the Last Passover meal between Jesus and His Apostles. Peter and John under instructions from Jesus have arrived in Jerusalem to make preparations for the Last Supper.

* See Hebrews 9:25, 9:26, 7:27, 10:11 (previous chapter)

From the death of Jesus onwards, He wished it to become a simple memorial supper. Jesus and the remaining 10 Apostles arrive to join Peter and John. The sun is sinking on the horizon as Jesus and His Apostles descend the Mount of Olives then they all meet in the home in Jerusalem, where the celebration of the customary passover feast or Jesus' 'Last Supper' takes place.

The exact form of words Jesus used over the bread and wine vary in the Gospels. Some scholars consider Pauls version at 1Cor. 11:25 *"This cup is the New Covenant in my Blood"*, more likely to be original on the Assumption that Jesus would never have suggested that His Apostles should drink His Blood as Mark 14:24 suggests. So between scholars there is a debate and its inconclusive.

But whatever view from the Bible writers is grasped - the **New Concise Bible Dictionary** (Lion -1989) states the following (page 321). *"There is however little doubt that a literal interpretation - 'this is (literally) my blood' - is ruled out on* *linguistic grounds. Jesus was speaking figuratively."* And long before the Last Supper Jesus blessed bread and broke it just as at the Last Passover meal. This was simply an act of Communion (an act of sharing) to feed His hungry disciples and the people, two accounts of such are found at Mark 6:41 and Mark 8:6.

Traditionally wine had always been used for the Passover meals. There is no mention in the Bible that the Apostles from the time of Jesus "Last Supper" ever kept the command from Jesus to commemorate His death. But we can be fairly certain they would have done, as it was a command from Jesus (or a request). And if it was done it's fairly certain it was at Passover the Memorial of Jesus' death. Paul at 1 Corinthians 5:7,8 gives good support to this belief when he says:- *"For Christ our Passover Lamb has been sacrificed. Therefore let us keep the festival . . . with bread without yeast, the bread of sincerity and truth".*

Jesus did not tell His Apostles in the upper room, how often to eat the bread or drink the wine in memory of His death. But however as the memorial was instituted on the date of the

Jewish Passover, which was replaced for His Disciples (and all Christians) by the memorial of Christ's death, and again taking what Paul wrote at 1Cor 5:7,8 - again it can be safely concluded it was to be an annual event.

So again to say as noted earlier breaking of bread was done for many occasions in the time of Jesus. It was done by Jesus to feed His Disciples and the people in the desert region. It was done by the Jews, after they had devoted themselves to the Apostles' teaching. It was done by Jesus at the Last Supper. In all cases it was just a simple meal.

The bread of course as the wine were changed in no mysterious way. If the bread and wine were to be changed in some miraculous way, the Apostles with Jesus in the Upper Room would of course have been told about it. The simple rule again if it's in the Bible it was to be, if not it was not. The Apostles were of course not cannibals they would not have eaten anybody in the literal sense or drank their blood.

The Apostles knew also that Jesus would give *"His Body once and For all Time"*. So on death

Jesus old physical body was gone for ever. His blood mixed with water had come from His side, to fall at the foot of the cross at a place called Golgotha or Skull place. It was all done for you, one great ultimate sacrifice, so that you and all your loved ones could live again on Resurrection.

Jesus body and blood were sacrificed forever for you. One could not eat them even if they wanted to - His body was gone, His blood soaked into the ground. Jesus did not have to give his literal body or blood for you anymore. There was no need to look for them back so as you could eat and drink them.

So when Jesus, said at the Last Supper as He broke bread *'Take it and Eat;' 'This is my body.'* What did he mean? And when Jesus said to them as He took the cup with wine *'Drink all of you from this, for this is my blood, the blood of the covenant, which is to be poured out for many for the forgiveness of sins"*. What did Jesus mean here? He also talks about eating His flesh and drinking his Blood at John 6:53-57. Again what's meant by it?

The bread for starters symbolised His own sinless body of flesh. This, He was giving for the future life prospects of mankind. The wine also symbolised his own lifeblood. By means of his shed blood, forgiveness of sins would be possible for those who put faith in it. So at this stage an infant would know that Jesus said and meant at the Last Supper. What Jesus had in mind of course as the **New Concise Bible Dictionary** has stated already was eating His body and drinking His blood in the figurative sense.

And when early Christians met they would have exactly done that by putting their faith in the ransom sacrifice of Jesus, just as we Christians when it comes to the Memorial of the death of Jesus do today. By putting your faith simply in the body and blood of Jesus who was sacrificed for you is enough. When Jesus spoke how people will get everlasting life, what did he say was the will of His father? It was as follows *"that everyone who beholds the son and exercises faith in Him should have everlasting life."* Nothing can be clearer than that. Then it's logical to say that anyone *"eating His Body and Drinking His blood"* in the figurative sense, and exercising faith in their redeeming power (that great sacrifice) will be resurrected to a new life.

It was a Sunday mass in 1995 in the suburb of Sutton (Dublin). But on this occasion a RTE camera crew were present, to film the 10.30 mass. But then an incident happened. This resulted in the Curate Ciaran O'Carroll having to wipe away his tears and admit *"The reality is we are all sinners" Romans 3:23*. Do you believe men like that *"sinners"* as we all are, have power to turn ordinary wine into blood?

The early christians right up to the Fourth Latern Council had no 'Transubstantiation' act. This act was thought up by Pope Innocent III (1198 AD-1216). So what do you think will happen to all the Christians up to that date? What did Jesus tell his Apostles?

Brian Darcy, a Vatican spokesman, on most Vatican issues - including 'celibacy' and 'Transubstantiation' and so on, says of Transubstantiation the following, "wine is changed into the precious blood". But then Brian seems to doubt his *powers* - Brian tells you it has the *"characteristics"* of wine once you drink it!

Now it's either blood or wine after 'Transubstantiation' don't you agree?

Brian Darcy now believes the potential for priests to be over the legal limit on altar wine alone is greater than ever. Altar wine is quite strong and even alcoholic priests for a valid mass are made drink it by Rome! They must also drink the contents left over by their Ministers of the Eucharist. Now they are afraid of the drink driving laws in Ireland in 2008.

CELIBACY AND PRIESTS

The man tipped to be the next head of the Catholic Church in England and Wales reignited the debate on celibacy within the Roman Christian Church in 2008. Malcolm McMahon was the Bishop in question. He believes married men should be allowed to become Priests. Pope Benedict XVI reaffirmed the value of 'celibacy' in 2006.

Celibacy was only introduced to the Catholic Church in the 11th century, following a decree by Pope Gregory VII. Malcolm is now afraid that people will be deprived of the Eucharist because of Priest shortage in 2008 - hence the celibacy debate again! Malcolm did caution that allowing Priests to marry "would create problems", and said that "supporting families would cause financial problems for his Church".

A survey carried out by Newstalk early in 2008 revealed that out of 100 Priests, 16% of Priests admitted to not being celibate. A further 24% refused to answer questions.

Celibacy putting it simply is a complete farce from the 11th century. Why is it only a farce? For starters the 100 Priests gave your answer. Also let the story of the Bishop and the American divorcee give you the answer. Let the story of the Priests from the "All Priests variety show" give you the answer. This show toured Ireland in the early 1980's.

So if celibacy was removed would Priests, and Bishops, etc., no longer have affairs? Believe that and you're just as likely to believe you will find a pot of gold at rainbows end! By means of 'celibacy' the Vatican saves its vast wealth. Remove celibacy the Pope's clergy would then have all the problems common to men.

The Vatican would find itself back in the free-wheeling days of the Borgia family. Rodrigo Borgia bought himself into office of Pope in 1492. He was called Pope Alexander VI. Alexander was Himself even embarrassed by his vast number of children. Once Rodrigo became Pope he commenced a campaign of diplomacy, assassination and treachery. For 24,000 Gold Pieces Rodrigo once sold a nobel man permission to commit incest with his sister.

So if celibacy was removed every one knows as in the case of Rodrigo (Pope Alexander VI) one would see a vast amount of children running around the Vatican and falling down its steps etc! The children would all be clinging on to the Cardinals and Bishops robes. People would be calling the priests; 'Father', and so would their own children of course. When the priest would hear the word 'Father' the poor man would of course not know where to look!

Then to add further to all this confusion as mentioned earlier the priests then like a lot of the rest of us would commit adultery, etc. Then that in return would lead to divorce and much more. Then who would support all the children from the cardinals, bishops, and priests in such circumstances? Would the Pope take money out of his IOR account to support them? Then the cardinals, priests, etc, finding themselves in a divorce situation, would have to buy new homes for themselves etc. Where would all that money come from? This very question has Malcolm McMahon very worried - in November 2008.

If Bishop Lee had to beg for money for his superior in 1994, what would he have to beg for then? At that time if one was innocent enough and believed William, one would have thought the Pope was struggling to keep the Vatican walls up! William said the demands on his superior were increasing each year. The result was a *"deficit"*. The Pope one would have thought was in danger of getting admitted to the "poor house".

So it's the reason the Popes will never abolish celibacy for their clergy. Of course its obvious to anyone in the real world - that the Popes love their vast wealth be it in money, massive resources in property, land, the list goes on and on. They of course would never be prepared to share it out with their clergy, when divorce problems etc arose for them. The cardinals, bishops, and all clergy in such circumstances, would end up running all over the place, with no homes or palaces to live in - what then?

Back in 1994 a priest by the name of Brian Darcy said of Himself as following - *"I am going through a long night of the soul"*. But then he went on to say *"I am missing what I have voluntarily given up"*.

Perhaps Brian should have listened his superior Sean Brady. Bishop Brady said in 1995 *"He regarded Celibacy as a great gift"*. As Brian Darcy said they take the vow *"voluntarily"*. No Spanish Inquisition, or no rack system, is used by the Vatican, to make them take their vow of celibacy. Again when they do how many of them keep it, if they don't want to?

The "Soul"

To find out how you became a "Soul" we have to go back some thousands of years. If a Christian it brings us back to the wonderful story of the biblical creation. If not it brings us back to some unknown time and the theory of Evolution. Millions today believe in Evolution, other millions in creation, others uncertain what to believe. Evolutionists contend creation is not scientific. Is Genesis just another ancient creation myth, as many contend?

Again this book is not a debate on either. The author of this book accepts "In the beginning God created the heaven and earth". If I am wrong it's a one way journey, it's as simple as that! I believe before the world was, there existed one great being whom we call God: uncreated, self-existent, all sufficient and eternal; who always was and always will be.

The usual Hebrew word for Soul occurs 755 times in The Old Testament, and has the primary meaning of possessing life. It was as you will note in the next chapter applied to humans (Adam) and animals. The initial occurrences of Ne'phesh

(Hebrew for soul) are found at Genesis 1:20-23. The Greek word for soul is psy-khe.

The big difference between humans and animals described as "Souls" in the Bible, is of course in Gods infinite purpose He planned the creation of man in his own image and likeness; and provided for man a suitable place to live - with animals in subjection. So man became a living "Soul" in the Garden of Eden. From the Garden of Eden man was to have domination over all the earth, as a living soul.

The principal geographical clue to the location of the Garden of Eden (original paradise) is the river that flowed out of it and divided to become four rivers. The third and fourth, The Tigris and Euphrates, still exist. The first two Pishon and Gihon are unknown, as is the exact location of the lands around which they flowed.

The **readers digest (illustrated guide to the Bible)** says "Regardless of its' location, the garden has come to symbolise an earthly paradise. In Hebrew Eden means delight, pleasure, luxuriance, conveying a sense of abundance and contentment". When the Hebrew Bible was translated into Greek, the word garden was translated as Paradeisos, meaning a park or formal garden. This word came into English as Paradise.

So it was in Paradise that the first human "Souls" lived. Paul as a Christian stated the first man Adam became a living **Soul** (1 Cor. 15,45). And it was in such a Paradise that Satan told our first parents, **they would not die if they disobeyed God**. Check your Bible and see what God told our first parents would happen? Remember the fallen Angel Satan, was an enemy of God. The next chapter answers how man becomes a living soul.

THE SOUL IMMORTAL?

In a funeral parlour in New York city, friends and family quietly file by the open casket of a 17 year old girl whose young life was cut short by a car accident. A clergyman tells her heartbroken parents "She is happier now", "God wanted her in heaven with Him". Do you believe this to be true?

Some 7,000 miles away, in Jamnager India, the eldest of three sons lights the wood on the cremation pyre for their dead father. Over the crackling of the fire, the Brahman chants the Sanskirt Mantra's: "May the soul that never dies continue in its efforts to become one with the ultimate reality".

Buddhists and some Christians leave the doors and windows wide open when a death in the household occurs. They believe that these measures facilitate the exit of the Soul. The teaching of the immortality of the Soul goes back to ancient Babylon. The result is nearly all religions advocate belief in the immortality of the Soul, but does this make it true? The Koran, The Holy Book of Islam, teaches that man has a

Soul that goes on living after death. So clearly religions around the world have developed a bewildering array of beliefs in the hereafter.

Clergyman **Harold S. Kushner** in his book **When Bad Things Happen To Good People** (1989) says at death the body "decays". But he believes "the Soul or personality does not". He said "But I am not capable of imagining what a Soul without a body looks like". He goes on to say **"Will we be able to recognise Disembodied Souls as being the people we have known and loved?"** This book was nominated by the Book Of The Month Club as one of the ten most influential books ever written.

John O'Donohue, author of an international best seller, says in his book **Divine Beauty** on the Soul - **"For your Soul then, death is a homecoming. Naturally the Soul will feel the sadness of withdrawal from the visible world"**.

Are we just flesh and blood? Or are we more than the sum total of the elements of which we are made? Are we here today and gone tomorrow? Or does some invisible part of us survive death and go on living? But nothing in scripture says we have some immaterial entity that lives on after death. People can search the bible to eternity and not once will they see written in it the word 'Immortal Soul'. Consider how the Bible describes the creation of animals Genesis 1:20,24 God said

"Let the earth put forth living souls according to their kinds, domestic animal and moving animal and wild bear of the earth."

Before that at Genesis 2:7 it says

"God proceeded to form the man out of the dust from the ground and to blow into his nostrils the breath of life and the man came to be a living soul."

Therefore as one can see all living creatures - humans or animals are souls. The bible's definition of *"soul"* is simple and consistent. The word can refer to a human or an animal. As we will see, this understanding harmonises with what the bible says happens to the soul at death. The Bible at Ezekiel 18:4 states *"the soul that is sinning - it itself will die"* God in Eden said to

Adam and Eve if they disobeyed *"you will positively die"* Satan said no they would "not die". If humans had an 'Immortal Soul' then Satan was right - just think about that. This was the first recorded lie in Eden from Satan. Jesus says at John 8:44

*"You are from your father the devil, and wish to do the desires of your father, that one was a manslayer when he began and he did not stand fast in the truth, because truth is not in Him when He speaks the lie, He speaks according to His own disposition, because He is a liar, **and the father of the Lie**."*

Here Jesus is telling that through the lie from Satan he became a manslayer. How is that one might ask? Well from that time onwards resulting from that lie that Adam and Eve believed mankind became a dying race.

Many of course believe the *"Father of the lie"* They believe they live on after death as a disembodied soul. In other words they die, but just a part of them (a shadowy part) that no one can describe - has some type of conscious existence. It's essential we take in the truth about what really happens at death. Jesus said at John 17:3

"*this means everlasting life, their taking in knowledge of you the only true God and the one whom you sent forth, Jesus Christ*".

Jesus was here telling true knowledge of God and Himself would lead to everlasting life in the Resurrection.

The revised standard version Catholic (Bible) edition (1965) says the following - (in its' explanatory notes) "As elsewhere (1 Cor 15:13-19) says survival after death is linked with the resurrection of the body". **The Lion handbook of Christian belief (1983)** says in its glossary - "Soul in the bible, this term is used for the whole self or person, body and mind. It does not mean some separate entity which separates from the rest at death. Christian immortality is an aspect of the whole person".

The New Concise Bible Dictionary (Lion-1989) says "the Christian **hope** for life beyond this is not based on a belief that some part of a person survives death. **Immortality is conferred by God**

and is attained through the ressurection of the whole person".

Again the Immortal Soul belief gives rise to many practices which the Bible call detestable to God, Spiritism, ouija boards, etc. The words of God tell you at Deuteronomy 18:10-12 - "*There should not be found in you, anyone who consults a spirit medium*" it also says "*or anyone who inquires of the Dead*". But sadly some persons are interested in such things, because they find it strange and mysterious, and hope they can contact the dead. But as you know now they go directly against God's command.

In 1926 one of the most famous magicians the world had known died - his name of course was Harry Houdini. During his life Harry had waged a campaign to show spiritualist for what they were frauds. Harry of course knew that no part of you survived death. When Harry knew he was dying, he and his wife Bess came up with a plan to counteract the fraudulent mediums.

Harry knew on account of his campaign against them, that they would let on they had contacted him, or let on they could 'Resurrect'

Him as it were. To prevent this Harry gave his wife Bess a secret code, that unless the mediums had it, Bess of course would know instantly they had not made contact with the great magician. For the next 10 years after Harry's death, mediums met with Bess every Halloween night to contact Harry. Did they contact Harry and give Bess the code - of course not they never did. So on the last Halloween night after 10 years, Bess said the following to the mediums - *"Harry is not coming back switch off the lights"*.

Lets go back to one of the most horrible deaths of all a Roman Crucifixion. The Romans had this horrible death perfected for such persons as criminals etc. But on this day one of the men to be crucified is no criminal, it's the Son of God Jesus Christ. It's Friday at a place called Golgotha, Jesus had been scourged and mocked the day before. But now it was time for Jesus to die in the most degrading form of execution.

Large crude iron nails used by Roman carpenters would have been driven through the wrists and feet to secure Him to the cross. The cross then would have been placed upright. Each breath Jesus took would have been excruciating. The last trust of a Roman lance through the side of Jesus would have caused blood and water to flow from the wound. It would have taken the greatest man who ever lived hours to die. The Roman army officer in charge of the execution was so over come by the death of Jesus as he stood near the cross that he gave glory to God. He was heard in his awe exclaim *"Certainly this was Gods Son"*.

Now ask yourself this, would God the Father allow His Son suffer such a revolting death so that you could live, if already, you were immortal anyway? If that was the case the horrible death of Jesus would simply have been a complete farce. **The Catholic Encyclopedia** 1991 states *"the soul is immortal"*. But what did God say to Adam and Eve in Eden? If they disobeyed God told them plainly and clearly at Genesis 3:19, *"For dust you are and to dust you will return"*.

Did God say to Adam and Eve if they disobeyed, it was still alright because on death they would live on in a far better place then the original paradise - so in reality you are not going to die Satan is right? And that in fact Satan had done them a great favour in Eden? And that Satan was not the "Father of the lie" as Jesus said? So what would that make the Son of God? God said back to dust, not right up here with myself in Heaven. If God wanted His human creatures in Heaven first day as shadowy souls, then there was no need to create the earth, the earth would simply have been a con job - it cannot be clearer.

But in Eden God had formed man and woman from the dust, man had lived from dust once, could He live again from dust in the future? If so who would make it possible? The man Jesus Christ who died an excruciating death for you at Golgotha of course. **The Family Encyclopedia of the Bible (Chancellor Press)** 1988 states on the 'soul', "the Bible sees human beings as a unity. It does not speak of an 'Immortal Soul' locked up in a decaying sinful body - this was a Greek pagan idea. Though it has been held by many Christians through the centuries."

The Encyclopedia goes on to say *"when we read the word soul in the Old and the New*

Testament", it means the whole of a persons being. When the psalmist says *"praise the Lord my soul"*. He is calling on himself as a *"whole person"*. Ezek 18:4 as you have read confirms the soul (you as a person) will die.

But the definition of someone as 'Immortal' would of course mean that person could never die, could never be destroyed is that not correct? Who is the only one mentioned in the bible as immortal? It's God of course, you can see this at **1 Timothy 6:16 when it says God** *"the one alone having immortality who dwells in unapproachable light"*.

And if you had an 'Immortal Soul' could God destroy it? But what does Jesus tell you at Matthew 10:28.

> *"Do not become fearful of those who kill the body but rather be in fear of him who can destroy both body and soul in Gehenna".*

(Some bibles here of course use the word hell). That proves what the Vatican call your 'Immortal Soul' can be destroyed. Now either a soul is immortal or not is that not correct? So what did

Jesus mean? He meant simply once we die, and unless God raised us from the dust and blow into our "Nostrils the breath of Life" we don't live again, we are destroyed as in Gehenna, annihilated, our bodies and future prospects of becoming a living Soul are destroyed.

Adam was formed from the same dust, then God gave him the *"Breath of Life"* and **Adam became a Living Soul (Being)**. Note the Bible doesn't say Adam was given a soul - but became one. So unless we are raised on resurrection with a new body and it's breath of life we as Jesus said are destroyed. But if God through the sacrifice of His Son puts the *"Breath of Life"* into a new created body, then you will become a living soul again just like Adam and Eve.

So as clearly stated and taking the main message of the Bible in its' context, man "came to be a living Soul". Hence man was a Soul, he did not have a Soul as something immaterial, invisible and intangible residing inside him. The Christian teaching of Paul did not differ from the Hebrew teaching (of Genesis) on the word "Soul" for man. Hence it sees the body plus its' "Breath of Life" needed to make the "Soul".

The Genesis account again tells you that a living Soul, results from the combination of the earthly body with the breath of life. The expression 'Breath of life' (literally breath of the Spirit, or active force of life) indicates that it is by breathing air (with its' oxygen) that the life force or "Spirit" in all creatures, man and animals, is sustained. The life force ("Spirit") is found in every cell of the creatures body.

So again you have learned God can destroy both **Soul** and **Body** in Gehenna. This again clearly shows that "Soul" (Ne'phesh - Psy-khen) does not refer to something immortal or indestructible. There is **not one** case in the entire scriptures, Hebrew and Greek which the word "Soul" is called immortal, indestructible, imperishable, Deathless or the like.

Some people who don't take the Bible in its' context might be confused by Ecclesiastes 12:7. It says here "The dust returns to the earth...and the spirit itself returns to the true God that gave it". So what does this mean?

The writer of Ecclesiastes did not mention that a disembodied shadowy 'soul' returns to

God at death. He did not mean the "spirit" was some vague, impersonal afterlife, an existence out of the body to follow death. The writer who spoke about the "spirit" returning to God at death, gave you the condition of the dead at Ecclesiastes 9:5 when he said -

"For the living knows that they will die,
But the dead know nothing".
(Once again death is simply a "sleep")

So what does the writer of Ecclesiastes mean about three chapters later? At death the life-force (Spirit) in time leaves all the body cells and the body begins to decay. But this of course does not mean that our life-force literally leaves the earth and travels through space to God. Remember your Soul is your body and life-force combined. The writer of Ecclesiastes agrees with the condition of the dead, "They know nothing" (they simply sleep).

The Spirit returns to God in the sense that now our hope for future life rests entirely with God. Only by His power can the spirit or life-force be given back so that we can live again on resurrection. Check your Bible for Psalm 104: 29, 30.

EVOLUTION OR CREATION?

Again either we accept we have a creator or if not of course it's simply the evolutionary theory! If it's by evolution we came, then we have no option but to accept the story offered by the natural sciences, namely, the evolution of the human race from simpler organisms, ultimately from a single living cell spawned in the earths' primeval oceans.

Then there is no more to come, its finished it's over, no resurrection hope. Because without Adam and Eve our first parents in this wonderful paradise earth as it was originally, then Jesus would not have had to die, then there was no resurrection. And then as Paul puts it at 1Cor:18, *'No Jesus, No Resurrection then all is 'Lost'"*. But I after years of study of evolution have accepted God as my creator, have accepted Adam and Eve my first parents, thus have accepted my only hope that on death a future resurrection.

If you accept evolution on the other hand, you accept that life began spontaneously elsewhere in the universe and survived under harsh conditions to reach the earth and later to develop into the complexity of life as we know it. This is one of the theories that life began in outer space. If it's the evolution theory which is held, it is reasonable that there should be at least some evidence to show that one kind of life turns into another kind. But the gaps between different types of life found in the fossil record as well as the gaps between different types of living things on earth today, still persist.

'Lucy' as we know was simply an ape. As we know scientists have turned to fraud in their desire to find evidence of 'Ape Men'. One example was the Piltdown man. The search for the missing link allows for speculation and myth to flourish. But simply fossil history doesn't agree with the evolutionary theory.

But do we have to search for Jesus like for the so called *"missing link"*? Of course not we know all about Jesus through sacred scripture. But outside the Bible is there any other proof that Jesus the man lived? The first century Roman historian Tacitus wrote *"The name Christian is derived from Christ who Pontius Pilate had executed in the reign of Tiberius"*. Also Pliny the younger and Suetonius also referred to Christ:

Flavius Josephus a first century Jewish Historian wrote of James, who he identified as the *"Brother of Jesus"*.

So early historians do mention Jesus, despite their references to Him are meagre. So with the Bible and their references we can be certain that Jesus did walk on earth. All the apostles witnessed for Jesus as he told them, some to the death. Paul before he became a Christian, was a Hebrew, a Pharisee. He had a commission from the chief priests in Jerusalem, all this promised Paul power and prestige, political and financial in the Jewish system. But what did Paul do? Remember He was once a convinced enemy of the Christian church. Paul of course gave all his power up to be a follower of Jesus the man he once persecuted. Paul to do that had to be 100% convinced in Jesus and the Resurrection, after all Paul died for that later and myths do not make martyrs!

THE SPIRITUAL DARKNESS I CAME FROM

It's sad to know many Christians live the greater part if not all of their lives in that condition. My definition of spiritual darkness would be as mentioned earlier as in the John Wesley story, a simple case of not knowing the truth relating to God and of his Son Jesus Christ. It's a case of calling ourselves 'Christian' while not as yet living in harmony with God's standards. It's a case of ignoring the basic principles that Jesus expressed. So we have a choice, be true or false.

During my religious studies in secondary school I would day dream as studies unfolded in the classroom, or almost doze off! How often in my subconscious mind did I hear the Brother in charge of religious studies ask, *"say the last word I said Mr. O'Brien"*. In many cases I did not know the first word, not alone the last! But despite that I was again really upset with my First Parents, knowing one day I had to die, on account of them believing the first lie in Eden.

Then I would go to Church, thinking I might find some knowledge there, but it never really happened. It was the same senseless mummery then and through the years, with the priests letting on they were converting the simple bread and wine into the actual *"Body and Blood of Christ"*. This may be what got me so interested in magic and Harry Houdini later. Basically I had gone to Church for many years of my life to search for enlightenment, but never found it. Then like Lord Byron who grew tired of life at an early age I grew tired of searching for enlightenment in Church. Lord Byron was tired of life when he wrote the following -

*"So we'll go no more a roving
So late into the night
Though the Heart be still as Loving
And the moon be still as bright."*

Byron was to die fighting for Greek Independence at the age of 36. His search for the Hedonistic Life had made him grow weary and tired. My search for God's true message as a young man had also made me grow weary and tired. In Byron's case it was to *"go no more a roving"*. In my case it was go no more to Church for spiritual enlightenment at least. I knew what I was hearing of hell, purgatory and a shadowy soul could not possibly be right.

I had searched for true information on the "Narrow Road" leading off into life but had not found it in Church. Then for years I was on the broad road, a road of darkness. But then through my love of reading, I found myself reading the Bible and many biblical aids, I liked what I read.

Then as I discovered it was the only source of true knowledge on God, it became compulsive reading and in return that led me to finding the truth that Jesus promised would set me free. The darkness was gone I had found the light.

PURGATORY

Firstly to confirm there's not a mention of the word 'Purgatory' in the Bible. It was simply an effort by the church to keep the superstitions multitudes through the ages under its control and terrified.

One can search the inspired words of God for ever, and not once will the word 'purgatory' be found. The Popes only formulated their doctrine on purgatory at the Council of Florence and trent. Up to that there was no purgatory!! The Council of Trent was plagued by interruptions. It started in 1543 and ran until 1563. Afterwards it took many years for its' decrees on 'purgatory' to be implemented.

The U.S. Catholic, March 1981, page 7, said "The Roman Church has relied on **tradition** to support a middle ground between Heaven and Hell".

They got their idea of purgatory from 1 Corinthians, chapter three, verses 10:15 - (1 Cor 3:10-15). Just because they saw words like fire and flames, 'wise guys' came up with their idea of 'purgatory'. Here it clearly talks of judgment day ("The Day"). The New American Bible says "Verse 15 has sometimes been used to support the **notion** of purgatory. Pope Paul VI (1963-1978) heaped praise on the New American Bible. He said of it "For the faithful... the New American Bible represents a notable achievement."

Purgatory as in the Sale of Indulgences, as in Limbo, was used and continues to be used to allow the Roman Christian Church to profit from fears of the people who don't know the truth. People believe by the payment of money to the church, they can free themselves by indulgences, and their dead loved ones from 'Purgatory'. It's by such means that the Vatican fills her coffers, to sustain its luxury and magnificence and the vices of some of its clergy.

The Catholic Encyclopedia on 'Purgatory' 1991 states - "It's a place where dead people wait who are temporarily and partially alienated from God by their sins". But the **new Catholic Encyclopedia** (1967 Vol Xl page 1,034)) states *"in the final analysis the Roman Catholic Church's teaching on purgatory is based on man made tradition not sacred scripture"*. So again either you want to cling onto man made traditions, or pagan *"Godless Myths"*, or accept the truth. I can only tell you the truth as contained in sacred scripture. I have found the truth, Jesus promised it would set me free, and it has. Free from all false fears and hopes.

Just remember you cannot purchase the Grace of God, but you are lucky because Jesus has done it for you. Jesus died for you in agony, resulting in that you can live on resurrection morning. In the Roman Church at this time, the myths of 'Purgatory' is high on the list as one of the most disgusting. Look at the **Concise Bible Dictionary** written by over 150 international scholars, not once will you see the word Purgatory, or the concept of it because they know it's not in the Bible - end of story.

The Catholic Encyclopedia (1991 page 800), has the following to say *"The Church do not specify the nature of the punishment of purgatory nor the duration of the punishment"*. Isn't that absolutely amazing! They have come up with the idea of purgatory, but know nothing of the 'Punishment' or for how long. Again they know nothing simply because its not there. We will go back to one man Cardinal Daly, who said again **the Bible is the only source of knowledge of God for us all, Popes, Cardinals, the lot of us.**

So again neither the word purgatory nor the idea of purgatory is found in the Bible. The **Catholic Encyclopedia** (1993 page 800) says "There are fires in purgatory". It goes on to say "These fires should be considered different from those of hell". Obviously they have sent one of their 'theologians' on an 'undercover' mission to find out this. Perhaps the stokers don't use the same premium coal! Perhaps they are not on the same pay scale as the stokers at hell! The encyclopedia goes on to admit the Greek Christians Church do not of course believe in purgatory.

Again the Vatican wilfully manipulate the words of sacred scripture for their own greed. Here at Corinthians 10:15 **The New American Bible** tells you "The Day" mentioned here is Judgment Day (of course). Corinthians talks of fire here. The American Bible says "Judgement Day will be either a time of gloom or joy". It will be a true test for us all, like straw going through fire. **The Bible says verse 15 "does not support** the notion of purgatory". It goes on to say "it does not envisage this". Again to confirm this **New American Bible** was highly praised by Pope Paul VI.

(Hades) Hell What Is It?

The World Book Dictionary for the word Hell says as following, *"In Roman Catholic and some other religions use, it's the place where wicked persons are punished after death."* If Hell really is a place of torment, you certainly should fear it. However if this teaching is not true, clergy who teach the doctrine (as purgatory) create confusion and cause needless mental anguish to those who believe them. Most importantly if not true such teachings defame God. **The Bible makes it very clear what result will wait for persons - who wilfully manipulate and distort the words of the Bible.**

The World Book give its own definition of Hell (Hades) as *"the abode of the dead"*, also as the *"Lower World"*. Now what are the abode of the dead, and the *"Lower World"*? They are both self explanatory - of course they mean mankind's common grave.

The World Dictionary said both also are called *"Hades"* and *"Sheol"*. In Hebrew Sheol is the word for the abode of the dead. But as one can see the World Dictionary says when both words,

Sheol and Hades are translated they mean the same grave. So from that it's quite clear that Hell is simply the *"Abode of the Dead"* or mankind's grave. The Catholic Encyclopedia admits to *"No explicit doctrine of Hell"*. The catechism of the Catholic Church says *"the teaching of the Church affirms the existence of Hell and its eternity"*.

Luke 16:19-31 speaks of a rich man, who "died and was buried; and in **Hades (Hell)** being in torment"...what was this all about? The story of the rich man and Lazarus is only an illustration or story. In the bible such stories are called Parables. In Aramaic 'Parable' also means 'riddle'. In the time of Jesus most of His hearers refused His message. Some of the Parables the disciples would have understood on their own, more times they asked Jesus to explain. They were all only like 'riddles' to the crowds who did not believe.

The New American Bible (Catholic) calls Parables "A short fictitious narrative from which moral or spiritual truth is drawn". The Pharasees who were listening to Jesus on the day he told the story of the rich man and Lazarus, had before that scoffed at Him. The rich man and Lazarus was to remain a 'riddle' to them, Parables were

Gods message to believers. **The illustrated introduction Explaining The Gospels** book says "obviously the details of this Parable are figurative". 'Abrahams side', 'The Great Chasm' and 'This Fire' are all apocalyptic images, not intended to teach physical realities.

Basically this Parable is about two classes of people - the rich and the poor. But this parable is teaching about those spiritually rich and those spiritually poor. They are symbolic classes of people, logically again their deaths were symbolic. The 'rich man' represented those already mentioned, The Pharasees, along with The Sadducees, The Scribes, and Chief Priests as well. The 'poor man' represented Jesus' disciples. The 'rich man' had denied Lazarus (poor man) spiritual knowledge. This changed at Pentecost 33ce, the 'poor man' then became spiritually rich. The 'poor man' then came into favour with God (The Greater Abraham).

The Pharasees and others were not to gain that position. It was their own fault, they were lovers of money, boastful, and were not to adhere to the teachings of Jesus. They had died to their once favoured seeming spiritual position. It's this that has the 'rich man' "in anguish in this flame". They had scoffed and sneered at the message of Jesus. They are now spoken of as being in figurative torment, as a result of dying to their former position of seeming favour.

Now just in case lets pick another Dictionary off my shelves to see how it defines Hell. This time I will go for **Websters** to see what it says. It says the very same as the **World Book Dictionary**. It says the English word *"Hell"* is equal to the Hebrew word Sheol, and again the same as the Greek word Hades - and what do the words Sheol and Hades mean again? Yes! Of course the abode of the dead - the grave.

So both dictionaries agree Hell is simply the grave, not a place of torment. The King James Bible translate the Hebrew word Sheol 31 times as Hell. They translate the Hebrew word Sheol 31 times as grave. They translate the word Sheol 3 times as pit. So it's ever so clear as the Bible agrees with both dictionaries, the English word Hell simply means the grave of mankind.

So the Greek word Hades, and the Hebrew word Sheol are confirmed by all to mean the same. At Genesis 37:35 when Jacob suspects his son Joseph has been killed, what does he want to do? He says the following *"I will go down to the grave"*. Jacob of course would have been talking in Hebrew, and would have used the word *"Sheol"*. Some Bibles here use the word grave, some use the word Hell. The New International Bible says as above *"I will go down to the Grave"*. So what did Jacob mean? It's logical, Jacob was overcome with grief thinking his son had been killed, so Jacob himself in his own grief simply wanted to die. He did not want to live after the 'death' of Joseph as he thought then.

The New International for the 3rd time as it's important translates Sheol here as grave, the **King James version** translates Sheol here also as grave. The **Douay version** translates Sheol here as Hell. Now a blind man can see the Bible Hell from your dictionaries and Bible means mans common's grave.

Now that you understand the English word Hell as translated from Sheol and Hades, lets move on a little further. Now you know Hell is not a fiery place of everlasting torment, but how did it get that Medieval Image? Jesus did of course use vivid symbolic language at times in the Bible, concerning the wicked, but persons who understood the Bible and did not take it out of context would know exactly what Jesus meant on such occasions. When it came to wicked persons in the Bible a lot of fiery symbolic language was used. But as one can now understand it certainly doesn't apply to the *"Bible Hell"*.

Now at least you will know what to believe when the Roman Church teach Jesus on death went to their man made 'Hell' - As I was taught by them. They get this idea at Acts 2:31 from the Christian Greek word Hades, and then they put fiery imaginary on it they get elsewhere from the Bible, to become their Vatican 'Hell'.

The word **Sheol** is found over sixty times in the Old Testament, when translated again of course means '**Netherworld**', '**lower world**', 'a**bode of the dead**', quite simply the grave.

People for hundreds of years have had images of "Hell" as a place where little devils with pitchforks hung out! The **family encyclopedia of** the Bible says; "The Hebrew word Sheol (and the Greek word Hades) translated into Hell means not a place of eternal punishment - but the place of the dead" (grave).

Three Christian Bibles have been picked to explain where Jesus went following his crucifixion. This will later bring us back to the Acts 2:31. The Catechism of the Catholic Church (page 144) says while Jesus went to the abode of the dead (Hades- Hell), He also went to a part of Hades where the dead were conscious, this is the Vatican teaching (their 'Hell').

For this 'Theology' they have to take 1 Peter 4:6 completely out of context. Peter here says "For this is why the Gospel was preached even to the dead". The Vatican will tell you Jesus spoke to those in Hades - (their man made 'Hell' on that day), what Peter said here had nothing at all of course to do with the day Jesus died. **The New American Bible** tells what Peter meant. Peter meant of course "Christians who had died since hearing the Gospel". It may also have included those spiritually dead.

Back to Acts 2:31, one Bible says of Jesus "His Soul was not left in Hell". Please note "His Soul" would mean the body of Jesus of course. **Jesus Himself at Matthew 12:40 had said "The Son of Man will be in the heart of the earth 3 days and 3 nights".** The heart of the earth was not paradise - or man made 'Hell'. It's self explanatory, it was in His grave or tomb.

The Bishops (Greek for overseers) when they wrote The 'Apostle's Creed' said of Jesus "He descended into Hades. The Popes then later as time passed, ignored what Jesus had spoken, and also put their own distortion on that simple Greek word Hades - and made it into their own man made 'Hell'. The Apostles Creed had nothing to do with the 12 apostles of course. It was not they that wrote The Creed. This was not written until around 200 A.D. The 12 Apostles as you know were long dead by then.

The New American Bible (1987) translates Hades at Acts 2:31 Netherworld. The New International Bible translates Hades at Acts 2:31 as Grave. (Just remember Hades would have been the original Greek word used). The revised standard version Bible uses the original word Hades. Take your time if you must to study this section on "Hades" - "Hell" and it will become crystal clear to you.

It took until the sixth century for the Popes to get established. The advancing centuries would witness an increase in distorted truths by Popes - "Hades" getting turned into their 'Hell' etc. Some of the early Popes practiced vice without restraint. Fraud, avarice and profligacy prevailed. 'Wise Guys' in some Christian Churches distorted the word "Hades" and its meaning for their own gains. Such teachings would terrify the superstitious multitudes. By such means of teaching 'Purgatory' and 'Hell' etc., Rome filled her coffers and got the wealth the Vatican has today.

Again, the 'Apostle's Creed' a classic summary of Christian belief, states that between Jesus burial and resurrection *"He descended into 'Hell'"*. This of course has always puzzled many people - why would the sinless Jesus be in the Vatican 'Hell' and not his tomb (Grave) the bible hell even if it was only temporary? Author J.

Stephen Lang says as you now also know - the problem is one of translation.

He says *"the creed written in Greek, says Christ descended into 'Hades', the Greek word for place of the dead, the Netherworld (grave) not a place of eternal punishment"*. He says it has the same meaning as the old Testament word Sheol. Your dictionaries and bibles quoted from will have confirmed this already for you. J. **Stephen Lang** says some churches try and correct this now by - simply omitting *"Descended into Hell"* from the creed. But Lang author of **the complete Book of bible Trivia**, and other Bible related books says - it's important the Churches replace it with *"descended into the realm of the dead"* (Grave, Tomb) *"Because this reminds us Jesus did indeed die a normal human death before God raised Him"*.

Because if Jesus was in the Vatican 'Hell', then he would not have been dead at all. So if Jesus was in the Vatican 'Hell' he did not die. Instead he simply went for a walk about to have a chat with the lads who were 'supposed' to be 'eternally damned', and also to check the central heating system, to know if it was hot enough for the inhabitants!

If Jesus was not in the Bible "Hell" (Hades) Paul tells you at 1 Corinthians 15:12-18, what the result would be. *"But if it is preached that Christ has been raised from the dead, how can some of you say that there is no resurrection of the dead? If there is no resurrection of the dead, then not even Christ has been raised. And if Christ has not been raised, our preaching is useless and so is your faith . . . For we have testified about God that He raised Christ from the dead. But if He did not raise Him if in fact the dead are not raised . . . You are still in your sins. Then those also who have fallen asleep in Christ are lost".*

So to put it so that a child can understand, Jesus had to be brought back from the Bible Hell (Hades), not from the Vatican 'Hell'. He was either dead or he wasn't, if he wasn't dead we are all on a one way journey, as paul said all is "Lost". This comes from a man who once had taken part in the fierce persecution of the Christians. But later was convinced so much of the death and resurrection of Jesus, that He allowed Himself in a position to be beheaded in the year 67 AD.

The Church of England reported in 1996 from the Doctrine Commission, *"That eternal torment in a flaming pit"* it is not biblical. They described Hell then as a state of *"**Annihilation**"*. This is partly true because if one is not raised from the dead, all as Paul said is *"Lost"*. You remain dead for ever, annihilated. The paper in 1996 also reported *"The study runs counter to attempts by the Church to play down Hell (The Church's Hell) and try to end a religion of fear in recent years"*. The paper also reported that *"In 1994 the former Bishop of Durham the Right Reverend David Jenkins completely rejected his church's man made Hell"*.

There was one bishop at least who had taken time off to discover some of the truth as contained in sacred scripture. So now you understand for even the most evil of men there is no man made 'Hell'. They now die as you and I for their sins. Now you say that's very unfair - but wait! On Judgment Day (Resurrection morning) you go off to live life in Paradise, and they go back to the *"symbolic everlasting fire"*. They go back to a state of being dead - back to their graves a state of total annihilation, no more Resurrection for them, punished for ever with everlasting death.

It's how the evil are justly rewarded, they pay the ultimate price for their evil - while you are rewarded with paradise and eternal life. You will then live on the New Kingdom we pray to come in the *"Our Father"*.

In the "Our Father" we ask God for His Kingdom to come where God's will is to be done on earth. One can clearly understand it's a Kingdom (Paradise) in the future to come. This was the Kingdom to come or the restored paradise, where Jesus promised the good thief he would live in the future. What Jesus said to the thief of course was "Truly I tell you today, you will be with me in paradise".

The understanding of some bibles of Luke 23:43 is influenced by the punctuation used by the translator. Some dictionaries confirm there was no punctuation in the original Greek bible manuscripts. **The clear teachings of Jesus and the rest of the bible must be the basis for determination**, and not a comma inserted centuries after Jesus spoke to the good thief. Jesus' words to the thief could not have been

"Truly I tell you, today you will be with me in paradise". One must not take the main bible message out of its' context. To do this is to defame the words of God. Again Jesus tells us what the result will be for persons who do so.

The Vatican through its' clergy teach that the thief was in heaven that day with Jesus, they also tell you Jesus went to their man made hell on that day. Jesus told Mary on resurrection morning - "Stop clinging to me for I have not as yet ascended to the Father". That was only to happen 40 days later.

If Jesus was in heaven, or the Vatican man made 'hell' on that day, then he was not dead at all. Then his crucifixion was all a con job. We then have in actual fact been told fairy tales, by 'clever' writers who lived a few thousand years ago. And if that's the case on our deaths, we have no more life to come, life just happened by evolution, it's as simple as that.

The Vatican through its clergy, will have Jesus in heaven (with the thief) and also going to their man made 'hell' on that day. They will have Jesus all over the place on that day!! Everywhere except where he was supposed to be. No death, then there was no resurrection, then Paul gives the answer.

GEHENA

Now you know the Bible Hell (Sheol, Hades) is just your grave where you sleep until Resurrection. But before you knew the truth did you ever stop and ask yourself how could a God of *"Love"* create a place as the Roman Church make up to torment evil people for ever? To torment a person forever as some Churches teach, just because He did wrong on Earth for a number of years would of course be contrary to God and Justice. God is a God of love, not hate. We as humans are told to forgive our brother indefinitely by Jesus.

So what if we as mere humans have that command from Jesus, what does that say we can expect from God but Love and forgiveness if we repent. After all that was the reason Jesus died for us. He died for all mankind; So could a God of Love torment people forever? Of course not! now you can see from that point alone how distorted the Vatican 'Hell' doctrine is. John 3:16 tells you *"For God loved the world so much that He gave His only begotten Son"*.

But did Jesus not use fire and brimstone talk when it came to the wicked? Of course he did and I am glad you know your Bible to that extent. It's exactly how some Churches have distorted the Bible truth and taken it out of context. It all started from a fiery place with plenty of brimstone and sulfur that did exist in the time of Jesus and long before that.

Must I really tell you how the Roman Catholic Church for one took the characteristics of a place that did exist on earth, a very fiery place, and made it into their hell? It came from a Greek word Gehenna that they took the liberty to render it by the word Hell. Actually I was hoping I could pass on it because I hate the smell of sulfur! But you have forced my hand so here goes.

So firstly to explain where and what was Gehenna? It was a valley outside the walls of Jerusalem, where Pagan Israelites who had not known God of course, sacrificed their children in the fires that burned there to their Pagan Gods. But a 2 Kings 23:10 you will read how good King Josiah made it unfit for such a horrible practice, instead turning into a huge garbage dump. But it was still there in the time of Jesus also as a dump to burn rubbish. Added to this dump to burn the rubbish and carcasses of animals, was brimstone (sulfur), I can even feel the heat now myself!

So whatever rubbish or carcasses went into this fire it was burned and gone forever of course, annihilated, end of story. At Mat 23:33 Jesus told the wicked leaders "Serpents, offspring of vipers, how are you to flee from the judgement of Gehenna" So what did Jesus mean? Jesus plainly did not mean the leaders would be tormented forever. But for Jesus anything that went into Gehenna was gone destroyed forever. Jesus in effect was telling the leaders once they were gone, they were gone, if they went to the symbolic Gehenna.

If that happened it was death, no life to come, like the rubbish that was burned gone forever. Jesus was using Gehena as a fitting symbol of complete and everlasting destruction. The name Gehenna appears 12 times in the Christian Greek scriptures. But as I told you many Bible translators put the word Hell in for Gehenna. John in the Book of Revelation also uses fiery symbolic language at Rev 20:13-15.

"and the sea gave up those dead in it, and death and hades gave up those dead in them, and they were judged individually according to their deeds. And death and hades were hurled into the lake of fire, this means the second death, the lake of fire. Furthermore whoever was not found written in the Book of Life was hurled into the Lake of Fire".

So what was John talking about? Well it is obvious, he was talking about Judgement Day. What does he mean by death and Hades gave up those dead in them? What have you learned Hades and Sheol meant from your lesson hell? Hades you learned was the grave. So basically John meant death and the grave were defeated for the righteous. But for those not on the Book of Life the unrighteous, what happens to them?

They are put into the Lake of Fire. What does John tell you the Lake of Fire is? Well just before I answer that it's the same as fiery Gehenna, the everlasting fire, *"unquenchable fire"*, *"eternal fire"*. All of them are symbolic references to annihilation as used by Jesus and others in the Bible to show the end result for those *"not written in the Book of Life"*. So John tells you what the *"Lake of Fire"* and all other symbolic references about fire in return - you are told quite clearly *"The second death"* (see Revelation 20:14,15). And just to prove the Lake of fire is symbolic. The Bible says *"Death and (Hades) Hell"* are thrown into it. Now of course Death and Hell cannot literally be burned. But they can and will be destroyed through Resurrection, Death and Hell (Grave, Hades) gone forever.

William Barclay in his book **Revelation** said "Finally, death and hades are thrown into the lake of fire". William was professor of Divinity and Biblical Criticism at the University of Glasgow. H.B Swete said "These voracious monsters (death and hades) who have devoured so many are in the end themselves destroyed".

Wilfred John Harrington O.P. studied theology at the University of St. Thomas, Rome. In 1993 he was a senior lecturer at Miltown Institute, Dublin. He has written extensively on both the old and new testaments. In his book **Revelation** he wrote "Evidently, Gehenna and the second death are one and the same". Wilfred said the 2nd death (lake of fire) is **Annihilation,** the final state of the wicked".

So briefly the first death is that we all have to die for original sin. Then there is going to be a resurrection of the righteous and the wicked. Then Judgement Day with the righteous and the wicked being judged. Then God says *"well done good and faithful servant, enter thou into the joy of the Lord".* To those not on the *"Book of Life"* God says "Depart from me you cursed into the everlasting fire".

So again as the *"Lake of Fire". What is the "Everlasting Fire"?* It's the second death as John told you, and if you understand your Bible and read it in its context, you will clearly then understand. Just imagine if the wicked were to live on in some fiery abode, Satan would still have been right in Eden - they would not have died. Satan would not have been *"The Father of the Lie"* as Jesus said.

The righteous die once are raised as promised to live in paradise. Peter calls this the New Earth at 2 Peter 3:13. Peter says

"But in keeping with his promise we are looking forward to a new Heaven and a new Earth, which will be the home of the righteous".

Then as Rev 21:5 says *"He will wipe away every tear from their eyes, and death shall be not more, neither shall there be mourning nor crying, nor pain anymore, for the former things have passed away".* The Catechism of the Catholic Church, 1994, pages 238-239 (Veritas) - states "the universe, then itself is destined to be transformed, so that the world itself is restored to its original state". They clearly talk about the *"New Earth"* on page 238-239 that is to come. The original state was paradise as you know now. Isaiah 65:17 also promises you the *"New Heavens and New Earth"* as Peter.

BETHANY

Now we come to a stage where we are no longer ensnared with lies. Romans 1:25 says "they exchanged the truth of God for a lie". We are not afraid of distorted truth, Acts 20:30. Paul warned even from their own group, men would do this. Like Marshal Ney you are now perhaps not afraid of the "sleep" of death.

You die for your sins, that's it. There is no Roman Catholic man made 'Hell' only Hell as in your grave. You know what fire and brimstone in the Bible mean, and where the words originated from. You know you don't have to be scared of so called 'Immortal Souls' you once believed existed as a shadowy figure in such places as the Roman Church purgatory. Before I found the truth this Greek pagan idea (originally) of a shadowy soul always frightened me anyway.

Years ago I would go to some ones home, after a family member of theirs died, to offer my condolences. But then returning home (and it was mostly walking for myself in the early 60's) I would always have found myself looking over my shoulder to see if the dead person was behind me! It was always such a scary feeling, thinking an 'Immortal Soul' could jump out of any part of the fence at me. But I suppose I should have known in those days, through my love of magic, and having great admiration for Harry Houdini, and knowing his life story, that no 'Soul' could come back and haunt me.

But in them early days I had not found the truth of course from the Bible. If Harry had managed to come back it would have been the greatest act ever he performed. But Harry knew as he lived there was nothing to come back, until resurrection. Every one of the 10 years that Bess and the mediums met after Harry's death, there was no response from Harry, just an empty silence.

But I could never figure out if 'Souls' were in Heaven or Purgatory in conscious form as thought by the Vatican and some other Christian Churches, and were aware of all that took place on earth, and especially with their loved ones, how could it have been a source of happiness or heavenly bliss to them to know the troubles of the living? If they were to witness the sins committed by their own loved ones, and to see them enduring all the sorrows, disappointments and anguish of life? How much of Heavens bliss would be enjoyed by those who were hovering over me on earth I thought? Now lets got to Bethany.

Lazarus and his sisters Martha and Mary were very good friends of Jesus. During the course of his Judean Ministry he would have visited their home many times. The bible tells the lovely story of the day Jesus visited them and Martha got involved in preparing a meal for Jesus. but what did Mary do? She sat herself down at the feet of Jesus and listened to him. Martha asked Jesus to tell Mary to help her. Jesus did not say anything to Mary, but used it as an opportunity to counsel Martha instead about the pressures of life. Later in the Bible it tells of the time a messenger ran to meet Jesus one day. What was his message?

It was of course to tell Jesus Lazarus was sick. Jesus remained two further days preaching where he was. Then Jesus told his disciples Lazarus was gone to *"sleep"*. He said *"Lazarus our friend has gone to rest, but I am journeying there to awaken him from sleep"*. So why did Jesus say Lazarus was only sleeping when really he had died? When they neared Bethany village Martha ran out to meet Jesus in her grief. Jesus then told Martha Lazarus would live again. Martha in return told Jesus she knew he would on ressurection, so obviously Jesus had told her all what happens at death, perhaps on the day the bible tells the story of Mary cooking while Martha sat at his feet to listen to Jesus.

Martha as one can see had one hope, it wasn't of an 'immortal soul' if it was she would have said it. Her only hope as Jesus would have told her Resurrection. Martha then called her sister Mary who then ran to Jesus and said to him *"Lord if you had been here my brother would not have died"* Mary was weeping sadness when she said this. Why did Jesus not tell Mary not to worry, don't be so sad because Lazarus was living in a far better place as an 'Immortal Soul'?

Remember Lazarus condition of four days was dead. So again had he been in Heaven as your Church teaches as a soul? And if not why not? After all Lazarus was a very good man, he was a very dear friend of Jesus along with his sisters. If Lazarus as good man was living as a 'soul' in Heaven, surrounded by Heavenly bliss, then would it have been right for Jesus to take him out of that and back to earth only to die again later?

And on returning it would have been the first thing Lazarus told his sisters, but of course you and I know now it was not the case.

You know now because you have read my book carefully and you have found the truth, and as Jesus told you it has set you free - free from all false hopes and fears. But remember Jesus at first told his disciples that Lazarus was only sleeping when in fact he was dead, again why was that? The apostles at that stage did not understand clearly enough what sleeping in death meant. So Jesus then had to tell them in a way that they would understand, and that was to say Lazarus was dead.

Before returning to Bethany Jesus had told his disciples he was glad they were not there when Lazarus died. Why did Jesus say this? Jesus gave the answer and what was that? John 11:15 gives the answer "So that you may believe". What did Jesus want them to believe? It was to prove to His Apostles that Lazarus could be awakened from the "Sleep of Death. To prove to His

Apostles a Resurrection was possible for those sleeping in death. Over and over the Bible calls death merely a "sleep". Jesus clearly had to die so we could live again, he clearly had to pay the only sacrifice ever needed and that was to lay down his life for us tortured to Death on a Roman Cross.

If the life of Jesus was not needed as the ultimate sacrifice for people to live again, then you would believe all people from Old Testament times were living as shadowy souls in Heaven, would you not? And if they were all living in Heaven, men like Moses, Jacob, etc. and women like Ruth, Naomi, etc., why would God allow the torture of His son to give life to people in a Resurrection, if already they had life without it?

Jesus said clearly at John 3:13 "No man has ascended into Heaven but He that decended from Heaven, the son of man". Therefore according to Jesus' own words, no one had gone to Heaven for those 4000 years of history (since Adam and Eve) down until his day. Jesus told you clearly he was the first. The Bible tells you also at Acts 2:29, 34. When it says "Actually David did not ascend to the Heaven". That is clear enough for all to see. So David of course on death did not go to Heaven.

But Jesus did tell some they would go to Heaven, a *"Little Flock"*, who were they? They were the Apostles that Jesus loved. Paul also believed his *"citizenship"* was to be in Heaven. Phil, 3:20. Jesus told his Apostles they would be in his *"Father's House"* Heaven - John 14:2. So the Apostles and Paul and the rest of the *"Little Flock"* (bible "Holy ones" or "saints") were to have immortal souls after all?

The following now is one of the most important Bible truths on having an 'Immortal Soul' to be learned. It's imperative to remember and understand the following. They would go to Heaven not at the moment of their deaths - but only when Jesus "Came again" - John 14:3.

Jesus had told them clearly they would go to Heaven - but again not until he returned. Paul also believed his *"Citizenship"* was in Heaven as noted earlier along with the Apostles and the remaining *"Little Flock"*. But Paul knew at first it was the *"sleep"* of death for him. Paul knew he would *"somehow have to attain to the*

Resurrection from the dead" - before he could get to Heaven as a spirit person like Jesus. Philippians 3:11.

So the Apostles and the rest of the "saints" knew it was not Heaven as disembodied souls the moment they died. Jesus told them He would have to *"come again"* and as Paul said he would have *"to attain to the Resurrection."*

So Jesus returns at their Resurrection of course - and then it's Heaven for just the selected few. Then and only then would their bodies be transformed like the *"Glorious Body"* of Jesus - Philippians 3:21. Jesus died with his physical body - after his *"sleep of death"* was resurrected and 40 days later entered Heaven as a spirit person.

It's to be the same with the Bible "saints" or *"Holy Ones"*. After their sleep of Death they will be resurrected when Jesus *"Comes again"*, and enter Heaven as spirit persons like Jesus. They will then carry out their roles as "saints" or *"Holy ones"*. They go to Heaven but it's for a specific purpose. Check out revelation 5:10, and 1 Corinthians 6:2 to see what that purpose is? They also of course will be part of the "New Heavens".

Just as we who will live on paradise earth will be part of the *"New Earth"*. Check out Isaiah 65:17, Isaiah 66:22 and 2 peter 3:13. Be like the bereans check and see what you have been told is true or false. Humans on earth who have been (like the Apostles and Paul etc.) set apart for the service of God are in the Bible called *"saints"* or *"Holy ones"*. Psalm 34:9. Acts 9:13. Romans 1:7, etc.

Paul said it was sleep until the *trumpet blows, now what could be clearer then that?* So with the *"holy ones"* in Heaven to rule with God through Jesus over the rest of us, this is the *"New Heavens and new Earth"* that Peter talks about at 2 Peter 3:13. And as Peter mentioned they will be the place of *"Righteousness"*. Also at Isaiah 65:17 God says *"For here I am creating a new Heavens and a New Earth"*. John also at Rev. 21:1-4 speaks of the New Heaven and a New Earth.

God's original plan of having the Earth as a paradise for us to live on will not then have been thwarted by Satan. The **"New Earth"** paradise restored will be our new home on Resurrection. God's word at psalm 37:29 says *"the righteous themselves will possess the earth and will reside on it forever."* Matthew 5:5 *"Blessed are the meek,* *for they shall inherit the Earth"*. Can God's word be any clearer then that for you?

So Paradise will be restored, with "No more wars" (psalm 46: 8,9) Crime and Violence, Gone for ever (proverbs 2:22), All humankind at peace (psalm 72: 7,8), No more famine (psalm 72: 16; 67:6) The dead all brought back to life (John 5:28, 29), Revelation 20:13. No more sickness or old age (Isaiah 35: 5,6 Revelation 21: 3,4). You again all know why you must die or fall asleep in death. Again its all down to our first parents of course. Our first parents believed the *"Father of the Lie",* result was humanity became a dying race.

WHO WAS SCRIPTURE WRITTEN FOR?

Sacred Scripture was written by inspired writers to benefit all mankind who want to search for God. It was written so that you and I may grow in truth through reading it. It was written for artists, philosophers, scientists, the lost of us.

The Bible is simply a Book of Intrigue. The bible firstly is a book of divine guidance and inspiration. It's also entertaining, fascinating, educational, character building. It's a history book, it's a romance book, it's an adventure and tragedy book. It's an action and thrills book. It's a book of bravery, loyalty and most importantly faith. Almost every phase of life and thought is dealt within its pages. It contains beautiful stories, biographies, letters, orations and much else. So it's easy to see even how a sinner like me got to read the bible and in return find the truth.

People find God in very many ways. I found him through my spiritual darkness and my search for the truth, and great love of reading. People can find God when adversity strikes in many ways. John Newton who was once involved in

African slave trading, found God as John Wesley through a storm at sea. At the height of the storm Newton called out for God's mercy, and was amazed to be saved from almost certain death. Yes! There was mercy, even for a great sinner like John Newton. Romans 10 verse 13 says "Whosever shall call upon the name of the Lord shall be saved". Newton renounced his involvement in slave-trading, and went on of course to write that great hymn *"Amazing Grace"*.

Abraham Lincoln the 16th President of the United States, called the bible, *"the best gift God has ever given to man ... but for it we would not know right from wrong"*. *Robert E. Lee (1807 - 1870) said "In all my perplexities and distresses the Bible has never failed to give me light and strength"*. The revised standard version Catholic edition 1965 says " *the bible is indeed for all christians a common source of inspiration and strength"*. So one can see quite clearly sacred scripture is written for all mankind who want to search for God, and accept God into his or her life.

It's imperative to remember one doesn't have to be a Pope or a Vatican Theologian to read, study and understand the Bible. The bible was written by some who were unschooled and ordinary men. The writers were among others a tent maker and a humble; fisherman. Acts 4:13 says *"when the saw the courage of Peter and John and realised that they were unschooled ordinary men"*. So to let on even for a moment one has to be a 'theologian' to understand the bible makes a complete mockery of sacred scripture. The World Book Dictionary 1979 describes Theology simply as *"the study of God and his relations with man and the Universe"*.

Literally, the word *"theology"* means *"science of God"*. One will see contributors to such books as the Catholic Encyclopedia, etc, describe themselves as following as having *"a doctorate in theology"*, *"A doctorate in moral theology"*, *"A master of divinity degree"*, *"A Professor of Systematic Theology*, *"A Doctorate in Sacramental Theology"*, *"A Doctorate in Sacred Theology"*.

Most of them also for a an extra little boost to their ego, also like to claim degrees in philosophy.

And all this just to understand the writings of some who were *"unschooled and ordinary"!!*

Thankfully you now know the Bible was written just for you. One certainly doesn't have to be a so called Professor of Systematic 'Theology'. To understand its main message the Bible is though designed to be studied carefully. You must be diligent in the study of God's inspired word. It's been many years of diligent study and research that has enabled the author to write this book.

The scriptures abound with examples of those who put forth concerted efforts in seeking God. You also can do that. If you earnestly seek the truth of the Bible, then you must not conduct yourself in an indifferent, self sparing or indolent manner.

The "Sleep" of Death

One does not need to be afraid of death, when one knows the truth. Like Marshal Ney I too can say *"I do not fear death"*. Of course I do not want to leave my home (earth) that God created me for. But like the poet I too know I've a rendezvous with death, and I also know I will not fail that rendezvous. But I know my *"Rock"* died so I could live again. Augustus Montague Toplady wrote a Famous Hymn about this same *"Rock"*.

"Rock of Ages, cleft for me,
Let me hide myself in thee;
Let the water and the blood,
From thy riven side which flowed,
Be of sin the double cure,
Cleanse me from its guilt and power".

So I also know of this *"Rock"* and how much he loved me a sinner, that he gave His life for me, the one and only sacrifice I would ever need so that I could live again on Resurrection morning.

Toplady knew he was cleansed from the power of sin, set free from the power of (Hell, Sheol,

Hades) the grave by his *"rock"* also. An American Civil war poem called the blue and the grey goes as follows -

"By the flow of the Inland river,
Whence the fleets of iron have fled
Where the blades of the grave - grass
quiver,
Asleep are the ranks of the dead:
Under the sod and the dew;
Waiting the Judgment day,
Under the one, the blue,
Under the other the grey".

This poem by Francis Miles Finch, states exactly the state of the dead. **They wait, resting in peace**. They sleep like all the famous people listed at the start of the book , who died at the height of their careers. Did that poet keep his pledge word about not failing His rendezvous with death? Of course he did! The poets name was Alan Seeger, and he kept his pledge word during a World War 1 battle in 1916. He was last seen alive urging on His fellow soldiers, the next morning his body was found in a shell hole. Alan had his rendezvous "On some scarred slope of Battered Hill".

So Alan from that war is sleeping, along with millions of others who fought in World War I. Many of them sleep in Flanders Fields, surrounded by poppies. The red poppies began to cover the battlefields of Flanders once the fighting had stopped. It is estimated as many as 21 million men, women and children lost their lives in that war.

But we need not fear death as Paul said at 1 Corinthians 15:26 "The last enemy to be abolished is death" Why could Paul be so sure of that? Because Paul had been taught by one who had been raised from the dead Jesus Christ. John 5:28.29 says *"the hour is coming in which all those in the memorial tombs (Hell, Sheol, Hades, Grave) will hear his voice and come out, those who did good things to a resurrection of life"*.

How could one come out to life, if as already stated in this book that life was there already in some type of 'Immortal Soul' form? Surely children in primary class could understand that one, as we are not talking rocket science. We are talking in straight language directly from the Bible, not a distorted untruth.

God, as you have already learned, started our first parents off in a lovely garden (Paradise) which was somewhere in the Middle East, as it's safe to conclude from descriptions given. That original Paradise plan was thwarted by Satan and the first lie. But God has promised to restore that Paradise to us on Resurrection when his Kingdom we pray for in the Our Father comes Matt 6:10. Then only the will of God will be done on earth. Have you ever asked yourself to picture what this creepy image of your shadowy soul might look like? Is is not many times easier to picture yourself in the body you were created to live on Earth with? Yes! of course it's way easier by far and not spooky at all.

The dust you return to at death, did God make people to live from that dust before? Of course He did, He did it before for people to live on Earth and will do it again as promised on Resurrection for us all. In the restored Earth (New Earth) mentioned previously in this Book, you and I will live. It will be Paradise restored, where we can enjoy life without end, free from sickness and disease. Gone will be wars, hatred, racial, prejudice, ethnic violence etc. Now is not that a wonderful promise of God through the sacrifice of His son Jesus for you?

The greatest man as you know by now called death a mere "sleep". Ecclesiastes 9:5, 10 again tells you of the condition of the dead, it says, *"For the living know that they will die; But the dead know not anything"*. **BUT FOR THE DEAD WHO SLEEP BE IT FOR A SHORT TIME OR A LONG TIME WILL BE LIKE ONLY MOMENTS IN TIME. DEATH WILL BE ONLY LIKE SLEEPING AT NIGHT, AND AWAKENING IN THE MORNING. WE JUST WAKE UP OBLIVIOUS TO THE TIME PAST IN SLEEP.** To them Psalm 90:4 promises *"For a thousand years in your sight are like a day gone by, or like a watch in the night. Such is the sleep of death"*. **John Donne** the English poet wrote about death in his poem **Life and Death** as following

"One short sleep past, we wake eternally, and death shall be no more, death, thou shalt die".

No one wants to die, no matter how old they may be in human terms, if one has a healthy mind and free from pain, people whatever age they advance to just don't want to die. It's simply because originally we were supposed to live forever, without having to grow old and die. Again to repeat Ecclesiastes 3:11 says *"He has even put Eternity into their minds"*. Once again where do healthy normal people want to live forever? It is where they were created for and have become used to living, Here on Earth. Man was made for the Earth, and the Earth made for man, Is that not correct? So one can understand the poem of Dylan Thomas when it says -

"Do not go gently into that good night, old age should burn and rave at close of day; rage, rage against the dying of the light".

This poem was published in 1951. Thomas often wrote about love and death. He wrote this poem for his father at a time when his father was old, sick and nearing death. But at least now we know that the greatest getting up morning of all will happen for those sleeping in death. On this Resurrection morning I will meet all my loved ones, all my friends again. When I am called from my deep slumber, then will I know I have death defeated. Then as Marshal Ney said, there was no cause to fear death. Both He and I and all of you people, with all our loved ones will have defeated death forever.

Then as before we don't have to worry just as were getting dug in, that we were growing old and in time would die. We are all aware we only do a fraction of the things we want to do before the sleep of death calls us. On Resurrection I will have so much to do and see, that before I could only dream of, because time did not allow.

The Bible tells us clearly (God's word) no immortal soul, only Resurrection to come or nothing. As Paul said no Resurrection all is *"Lost"*. He did not say no Resurrection, it's still okay as you have got an *"Immortal Soul"*. Paul of course did not say that as he was a christian, and believed the promises of Jesus so much that he was to die for them later. Paul would not have died for Pagan Greek Myths.

So on Resurrection morning we all can say with death defeated, "Where O Death is your victory? Where O death is your sting?" What joy beyond compare, to meet all family again, mothers who lost their children will again have them, husbands and wives meeting, running to meet each other on Paradise. The mam and dad, grandparents, aunts and uncles, brothers and sisters, nieces and nephews, all family that we loved, or maybe some we did not meet as death had called them. Some of us did not get to know our grannys or grandads, all that though will be resolved on Resurrection morning.

The word Resurrection comes from a Greek word which literally means *"A standing up again"*. Then it will be the New Paradise as promised for us all.

In the Book **What Christians Believe** written by **John Balchin** (A lion manual) page 121 he says the following; *"The Bible promises that God will recreate the earth and that we will live with Him on it"*. *God will live with us in the sense that he will have His attention always on us in paradise from Heaven.* **The Presbyterian Life**, May 1, 1979, p. 35. Says of the 'Immortal Soul'. *"Immortality of the soul is a Greek notion formed in ancient mystery cults and elaborated by the Philosopher Plato"*.

So when I meet my mam again with all my loved ones we will not certainly be meeting as 'Shadowy Souls'. To even think of that for a moment is a revolting thought to me. Mam and I and all our loved ones will rise again from the dust as God has promised through His son Jesus Christ. I will know my mam instantly, her old body as my own will of course have returned to dust, so on Resurrection we of course will have new physical bodies. All the infirmities of our old bodies gone for ever. We will have the same personal identity, we will have the same personality as when we died. This time we will know we have all pains, infirmities, defeated for ever. All our old pains will be forgotten about.

Death for those judged righteous will be gone for ever. Again to confirm God's original purpose regarding the Earth will be carried out. No more will we be haunted by the fact how life is brief and precarious. No more as individuals will we see death looming before us. Resurrection will be so wonderful that we can only now surmise the details of joy that will be experienced. We can be certain it will be more wonderful than any or all our dreams.

It will be joy again beyond compare to run to my Mam and hold her again, and tell her how much I love her along, with my Dad and all my loved ones. It will be a day that all sorrow and sighing will have fled away. Now we will be together for ever. All what we could only briefly think of doing before, will all now be before us on Paradise Earth. Paradise Earth where Jesus promised the good thief He would also live. Weeping bereaved ones tears will be gone for ever. Then as already written in this chapter the words of Jesus will have come to be. **John 5:28,29 - here again Jesus says** *"Marvel not at this: For the hour is coming in which all that are in the graves (Memorial tombs) shall hear his voice and come out (forth); they that have done good (the just) into the Resurrection of Life".* **On Resurrection you come out to life from the "sleep" of death.**

And all this comes through the love of Jesus for all christians who believe the truth. Again what is that truth? It's simply that as sinners we all die, but through the greatest one and only sacrifice of Jesus we live. It was the greatest sacrifice of all, from the greatest man who ever lived. Again to remember he was tortured to death for you. He gave His life for you at Golgotha or Skull Place. How the heart of the Mother of Jesus was pierced through, as she watched her son hanging there just for you. As Jesus gasped for His breath, the Roman soldiers mockingly offered Him sour wine, but apparently holding it just beyond His parched lips. Jesus prayed for the Roman soldiers, He asked God to *"forgive them"*. He wrenched with pain as the nails tore His flesh and ligaments, with the weight of His body on the Cross.

If you believe any more sacrifices, other then the one at Golgotha are needed - you have just mocked the execution. You have just become like the passersby who began speaking abusively to Jesus as He hung on the Cross. They also on that day mocked Jesus. The greatest of all events in human history occurred in the reign of the Roman Caesar Augustus, when Jesus of Nazareth appeared on Earth and gave His life on our behalf.

The Vatican has clergy who are known to use the gains of their Church offerings for 'sacrifices' for all kinds of acts. In 2007 it emerged three Vatican priests were accused of the following - they had used offertory money to keep girlfriends, take gambling excursions, foreign holidays and buy property. They also set up a 'Business' called SHAG!

If one believes the Immortal 'Soul' teaching, then you are already in Heaven in conscious form enjoying your blissful surroundings long before Judgment Day, is that not correct? Well then what is the point of Judgment Day? (Resurrection Morning) Matthew 25:21 tells you what the master will say to the faithful (when the master returns) - "*well done Good and Faithful servant enter thou into the joy of the Lord*" is that not correct? But how could you enter into the joy, if you were already in the "*joy*" as an 'immortal soul' for long ages? Further on at Matthew chapter 25 verses 31 to 34 Jesus says - **ONLY when He arrives in "His glory" (Resurrection Morning) will the "sheep" be separated from the "goats".** The righteous only then go to their reward or the "wicked" to their punishment. Could Jesus have been any clearer?

The Pope still wants People to believe that faith was transferred from Christ and God ("The

Rock"), the foundation of the Christian Church, to the Pope of Rome. Resulting from this deception the Pope has adopted supremacy in One Christian Church. All true Christians are all equal in Christ as their leader, whatever denomination they come from. Christ died for us all. His Father is the solid "Rock" foundation of the one true Christian Church.

Before I leave you after a wonderful journey of searching for the truth, I would like to say the following. If this book through all the many Bible references I have included for you will set but just a few to freedom, then it will be all worthwhile. If this book with the many Bible references will just plant a few seeds of understanding and of knowing the truth into just a few minds, then my mission has been accomplished. And hopefully seeds of truth now planted will sprout for years to come. **At proverbs 12:19 it says** *"truthful lips last forever, but a lying tongue lasts only a moment"*. Thank you for coming on this journey with me.